A MEMOIR OF JANE AUSTEN

An important and revealing work, J. E. Austen-Leigh's memoir of his aunt has been unavailable to the modern reader for many years.

Written some fifty years after Jane Austen's death the book contains chapters on her background and family connections, her life at Steventon, Bath, Southampton and Chawton, and is the only published record by someone who knew her. This edition also includes the cancelled chapter of *Persuasion* and the account of *Sanditon* (originally entitled 'The Last Work'), both of which appeared as appendices to the first edition published in 1870.

A Memoir of Jane Austen is reprinted in the *Century Classics* with a new introduction by Fay Weldon, author of *Letters to Alice*, an account of Jane Austen as written to her niece and adaptor of *Pride and Prejudice* for the BBC television serial. Fay Weldon is also the author of many short story collections and novels, including *The Life and Loves of a She-Devil* and *The Heart of the Country*.

Also published in the Century Lives and Letters

The cover shows 'Portrait of Two Sisters' by Thomas
Richmond

A MEMOIR OF

JANE AUSTEN

BY HER NEPHEW
J. E. AUSTEN-LEIGH

With an Introduction by
FAY WELDON

Notes and Index by
R. W. CHAPMAN

CENTURY
London Melbourne Auckland Johannesburg

First published in 1870; reprinted in 1871.
This edition first published by Century in 1987, an imprint of
Century Hutchinson Ltd, Brookmount House, 62–65 Chandos Place, London WC2N 4NW

Century Hutchinson Australia Pty Ltd
PO Box 496, 16–22 Church Street, Hawthorn, Victoria 3122, Australia

Century Hutchinson New Zealand Limited
PO Box 40–086, Glenfield, Auckland 10, New Zealand

Century Hutchinson South Africa (Pty) Ltd
PO Box 337, Berglvei, 2012 South Africa

ISBN 0 7126 1702 7

CONTENTS

Portrait of Jane Austen

INTRODUCTION

The volume is, of course, more than a mere memoir of Jane Austen, though that would be rewarding enough. It is a look back over an urbane mid-Victorian shoulder to the customs and manners of Georgian times, and we must thank the Gods of chance and literature that James Edward Austen-Leigh who, just happening to be Jane Austen's nephew, also happened to take such an informed and lively interest in the changing face of England, and to write with the same kind of diligent clarity and descriptive grace as his more famous aunt. But perhaps these writing skills are inherited.

Jane Austen died in 1817, when Mr Austen-Leigh was a young man of twenty. He writes in 1867, fifty years after her death, and claims 'some indulgent allowance for the difficulty of recovering little facts and feelings which had been merged half a century deep in oblivion'. Some things, I imagine, he left purposefully forgotten. After the manner of his time, he will speak no ill of the dead. 'Many will care to know,' he writes, 'whether the moral rectitude, the correct taste and warm affections with which she invested her ideal characters . . . were actually exhibited by her. . . I can indeed bear witness that there was scarcely a charm in her most delightful character that was not a true reflection of her own sweet temper and loving heart.' Well, I beg leave to doubt the accuracy of the nephew's witness – suspecting, from the internal evidence of the novels, that Jane Austen was a much sharper, shrewder, unhappier woman than he allows – but never mind. Mr Austen-Leigh wished to protect his aunt's reputation, and did. He went as far as seemed proper to him into the gossip of personality, and probably even a little further. The writing of novels by mid-Victorian times had come to seem a seedy and slightly scandalous business, especially when undertaken by women, and no doubt in 1867 it seemed all the more necessary to stress his aunt's respectability and rectitude. 'We did not think of her as being clever [oh, unfeminine!] still less as being famous [oh, indiscreet!] but we valued her as one always kind, sympathising and amusing.' [As any aunt should be!] 'She is entirely free from the vulgarity, which is so offensive in some novels, of dwelling on the outward appendages of wealth or rank, as if they were things to which the writer was unaccustomed' [oh, gentility!] '. . . nor does she go lower than the Miss Steeles, Mr Elton, and John Thorpe, people of bad taste and underbred manners.' (oh, moderate! oh, saved!)

I do think that Mr Austen-Leigh, in his attempt to 'sketch out a fine outline' of his famous aunt's 'excellence' has, over the years, done her something of a disservice. His insistence upon her very 'genteelness', his thankfulness that she did 'not meddle with matters which she did not fully understand', his relief that her writing never touched upon politics, law or medicine, did rather relegate Jane Austen, in the public mind, to the ranks of the delicate lady novelists, rather than to the weighty front line of English literature, where she is now increasingly seen to belong. The Austen-Leigh memoir looms very large in the Austen industry – that steady flow of biography and essays, critical and fanciful, Freudian and Marxist; studies and commentaries, kind and unkind; suppositions, likely and unlikely, which are published year by year, and for which the public seems to have an insatiable appetite – if only because we have so very little other actual information about the manner of Jane Austen's life. Her nephew's memoirs, along with her brother Henry's brief biographical note, prefixed to a late edition of *Northanger Abbey*, a collection of minor letters, one rather bad portrait of her by her sister Cassandra, and a quilt stitched (badly) by the novelist when young is just about all we have.

Nevertheless, the real strength and importance of the memoir, to my mind, is the occasion it affords James Edward for 'observing many changes gradually effected in the manners and habits of society' in a subject which carries him back a hundred years or so. 'They may be little things, but time gives a certain importance to trifles, as it imparts a peculiar flavour to wine.' And so it does – and here we have such intriguing descriptions of balls, and etiquettes, and household manners, and how gentlemen 'used to do their own gardening' and how 'the early dinner hour used to render candlesticks unnecessary' and how gloves which were a little soiled were thought good enough for a country dance – and a thousand other scraps of information and delight which make the volume such a pleasure to read, and re-read.

The Austen-Leigh memoir was allowed to go out of print in 1926. It is greatly to Century Hutchinson's credit that they have rescued it from its temporary oblivion. The volume includes R. W. Chapman's Notes and Index, of particular interest to scholars, a discarded chapter of *Persuasion*, and extracts from the unfinished *Sanditon*. It is good to have it back on the shelves again.

Fay Weldon
March 1987

PREFACE.

The Memoir of my Aunt, Jane Austen,
has been received with more favour than I
had ventured to expect. The notices taken
of it in the periodical press, as well as letters
addressed to me by many with whom I am
not personally acquainted, show that an
unabated interest is still taken in every
particular that can be told about her. I am
thus encouraged not only to offer a Second
Edition of the Memoir, but also to enlarge it
with some additional matter which I might
have scrupled to intrude on the public if they
had not thus seemed to call for it. In the
present Edition, the narrative is somewhat
enlarged, and a few more letters are added ;
with a short specimen of her childish stories
The cancelled chapter of ' Persuasion ' is
given, in compliance with wishes both
publicly and privately expressed. A fragment of a story entitled ' The Watsons ' is

printed[1]; and extracts are given from a novel which she had begun a few months before her death; but the chief addition is a short tale never before published, called ' Lady Susan.'[1] I regret that the little which I have been able to add could not appear in my First Edition; as much of it was either unknown to me, or not at my command, when I first published; and I hope that I may claim some indulgent allowance for the difficulty of recovering little facts and feelings which had been merged half a century deep in oblivion.

NOVEMBER 17, 1870.

---

[1] [*The Watsons* and *Lady Susan* are not included in this reprint.]

CONTENTS.

CHAPTER I.

Contents.

Contents.

' He knew of no one but himself who was inclined to the work. This is no uncommon motive. A man sees something to be done, knows of no one who will do it but himself, and so is driven to the enterprise.'

HELPS' *Life of Columbus*, ch. i.

A MEMOIR

OF

JANE AUSTEN.

CHAPTER I.

*Introductory Remarks—Birth of Jane Austen—Her Family
Connections—Their Influence on her Writings.*

ORE than half a century has passed away since I, the youngest of the mourners,* attended the funeral of my dear aunt Jane in Winchester Cathedral; and now, in my old age, I am asked whether my memory will serve to rescue from oblivion any events of her life or any traits of her character to satisfy the enquiries of a generation of readers who have been born since she died. Of events her life was singularly barren : few changes and no great crisis

* I went to represent my father, who was too unwell to attend himself, and thus I was the only one of my generation present.

ever broke the smooth current of its course. Even her fame may be said to have been posthumous : it did not attain to any vigorous life till she had ceased to exist. Her talents did not introduce her to the notice of other writers, or connect her with the literary world, or in any degree pierce through the obscurity of her domestic retirement. I have therefore scarcely any materials for a detailed life of my aunt ; but I have a distinct recollection of her person and character ; and perhaps many may take an interest in a delineation, if any such can be drawn, of that prolific mind whence sprung the Dashwoods and Bennets, the Bertrams and Woodhouses, the Thorpes and Musgroves, who have been admitted as familiar guests to the firesides of so many families, and are known there as individually and intimately as if they were living neighbours. Many may care to know whether the moral rectitude, the correct taste, and the warm affections with which she invested her ideal characters, were really existing in the native source whence those ideas flowed, and were actually exhibited by her in the various relations of life. I can indeed bear witness that there was scarcely a charm in her most delightful characters that was not a true reflection of her own sweet temper and loving heart. I was young when we lost her ; but the impressions made on the young are deep, and though in the course of fifty years I have forgotten much, I have not forgotten that ' Aunt Jane ' was the delight of all her nephews and nieces. We did not think of her as being clever, still less as being famous; but we valued her as one always kind, sympathising, and amusing. To all this I am a living witness, but whether I can sketch out such a faint outline of this excellence as shall be perceptible to others may be reasonably doubted. Aided, however, by a few survivors * who knew her, I will not refuse to make the attempt. I am the more inclined to undertake the task from a conviction that, however little I may have to tell, no one else is left who could tell so much of her.

Jane Austen was born on December 16, 1775, at the Parsonage House of Steventon in Hampshire. Her father, the Rev. George Austen, was of a family long established in the neighbourhood of Tenterden and Sevenoaks in Kent. I believe that early in the seventeenth century they were clothiers. Hasted, in his history of Kent, says : ' The clothing business was exercised by persons who possessed most of the landed property in the Weald, insomuch that almost all the ancient families of these parts, now of large estates and genteel rank in life, and some of them ennobled by titles, are sprung from ancestors who

* My chief assistants have been my sisters, Mrs. B. Lefroy and Miss Austen, whose recollections of our aunt are, on some points, more vivid than my own. I have not only been indebted to their memory for facts, but have sometimes used their words. Indeed some passages towards the end of the work were entirely written by the latter.

I have also to thank some of my cousins, and especially the daughters of Admiral Charles Austen, for the use of letters and papers which had passed into their hands, without which this Memoir, scanty as it is, could not have been written.

have used this great staple manufacture, now
almost unknown here.' In his list of these families
Hasted places the Austens, and he adds that these
clothiers ' were usually called the Gray Coats of
Kent ; and were a body so numerous and united
that at county elections whoever had their vote and
interest was almost certain of being elected.' The
family still retains a badge of this origin ; for their
livery is of that peculiar mixture of light blue and
white called Kentish gray, which forms the facings
of the Kentish militia.

Mr. George Austen had lost both his parents
before he was nine years old. He inherited no
property from them ; but was happy in having a
kind uncle, Mr. Francis Austen, a successful lawyer
at Tunbridge, the ancestor of the Austens of
Kippington, who, though he had children of his own,
yet made liberal provision for his orphan nephew.
The boy received a good education at Tunbridge
School, whence he obtained a scholarship, and
subsequently a fellowship, at St. John's College,
Oxford. In 1764 he came into possession of the
two adjoining Rectories of Deane and Steventon
in Hampshire ; the former purchased for him by
his generous uncle Francis, the latter given by his
cousin Mr. Knight. This was no very gross case of
plurality, according to the ideas of that time, for the
two villages were little more than a mile apart,
and their united populations scarcely amounted
to three hundred. In the same year he married

Cassandra, youngest daughter of the Rev. Thomas
Leigh, of the family of Leighs of Warwickshire,
who, having been a fellow of All Souls, held the
College living of Harpsden, near Henley-upon-
Thames. Mr. Thomas Leigh was a younger brother
of Dr. Theophilus Leigh, a personage well known at
Oxford in his day, and his day was not a short one,
for he lived to be ninety, and held the Mastership
of Balliol College for above half a century. He was
a man more famous for his sayings than his doings,
overflowing with puns and witticisms and sharp
retorts ; but his most serious joke was his practical
one of living much longer than had been expected
or intended. He was a fellow of Corpus, and the
story is that the Balliol men, unable to agree in
electing one of their own number to the Mastership, chose him, partly under the idea that he was
in weak health and likely soon to cause another
vacancy. It was afterwards said that his long
incumbency had been a judgment on the Society
for having elected an *Out-College Man.** I imagine
that the front of Balliol towards Broad Street which
has recently been pulled down must have been
built, or at least restored, while he was Master, for
the Leigh arms were placed under the cornice at the
corner nearest to Trinity gates. The beautiful
building lately erected has destroyed this record,

---

* There seems to have been some doubt as to the validity of this
election ; for Hearne says that it was referred to the Visitor, who
confirmed it. (Hearne's *Diaries,* v. 2.)

and thus 'monuments themselves memorials need.'

His fame for witty and agreeable conversation extended beyond the bounds of the University. Mrs. Thrale, in a letter to Dr. Johnson, writes thus : ' Are you acquainted with Dr. Leigh,* the Master of Balliol College, and are you not delighted with his gaiety of manners and youthful vivacity, now that he is eighty-six years of age ? I never heard a more perfect or excellent pun than his, when some one told him how, in a late dispute among the Privy Councillors, the Lord Chancellor struck the table with such violence that he split it. " No, no, no," replied the Master ; " I can hardly persuade myself that he *split* the *table*, though I believe he *divided* the *Board*." '

Some of his sayings of course survive in family tradition. He was once calling on a gentleman notorious for never opening a book, who took him into a room overlooking the Bath Road, which was then a great thoroughfare for travellers of every class, saying rather pompously, ' This, Doctor, I call my study.' The Doctor, glancing his eye round the room, in which no books were to be seen, replied, ' And very well named too, sir, for you know Pope tells us, " The proper *study* of mankind is *Man*." ' When my father went to Oxford he was honoured with an invitation to dine with this dignified cousin.

* Mrs. Thrale writes Dr. *Lee*, but there can be no doubt of the identity of person.

Being a raw undergraduate, unaccustomed to the habits of the University, he was about to take off his gown, as if it were a great coat, when the old man, then considerably turned eighty, said, with a grim smile, ' Young man, you need not strip : we are not going to fight.' This humour remained in him so strongly to the last that he might almost have supplied Pope with another instance of ' the ruling passion strong in death,' for only three days before he expired, being told that an old acquaintance was lately married, having recovered from a long illness by eating eggs, and that the wits said that he had been egged on to matrimony, he immediately trumped the joke, saying, ' Then may the yoke sit easy on him.' I do not know from what common ancestor the Master of Balliol and his great-niece Jane Austen, with some others of the family, may have derived the keen sense of humour which they certainly possessed.

Mr. and Mrs. George Austen resided first at Deane, but removed in 1771 to Steventon, which was their residence for about thirty years. They commenced their married life with the charge of a little child, a son of the celebrated Warren Hastings, who had been committed to the care of Mr. Austen before his marriage, probably through the influence of his sister, Mrs. Hancock, whose husband at that time held some office under Hastings in India. Mr. Gleig, in his ' Life of Hastings,' says that his son George, the offspring of his first marriage, was sent to England in 1761 for his education, but that he had never been able to ascertain to whom this precious charge was entrusted, nor what became of him. I am able to state, from family tradition, that he died young, of what was then called putrid sore throat ; and that Mrs. Austen had become so much attached to him that she always declared that his death had been as great a grief to her as if he had been a child of her own.

About this time, the grandfather of Mary Russell Mitford, Dr. Russell, was Rector of the adjoining parish of Ashe ; so that the parents of two popular female writers must have been intimately acquainted with each other.

As my subject carries me back about a hundred years, it will afford occasions for observing many changes gradually effected in the manners and habits of society, which I may think it worth while to mention. They may be little things, but time gives a certain importance even to trifles, as it imparts a peculiar flavour to wine. The most ordinary articles of domestic life are looked on with some interest, if they are brought to light after being long buried ; and we feel a natural curiosity to know what was done and said by our forefathers, even though it may be nothing wiser or better than what we are daily doing or saying ourselves. Some of this generation may be little aware how many conveniences, now considered to be necessaries and matters of course, were unknown to their grandfathers and grandmothers. The lane between Deane and Steventon has long been as smooth as the best turnpike road; but when the family removed from the one residence to the other in 1771, it was a mere cart track, so cut up by deep ruts as to be impassable for a light carriage. Mrs. Austen, who was not then in strong health, performed the short journey on a feather-bed, placed upon some soft articles of furniture in the waggon which held their household goods. In those days it was not unusual to set men to work with shovel and pickaxe to fill up ruts and holes in roads seldom used by carriages, on such special occasions as a funeral or a wedding. Ignorance and coarseness of language also were still lingering even upon higher levels of society than might have been expected to retain such mists. About this time, a neighbouring squire, a man of many acres, referred the following difficulty to Mr. Austen's decision : ' You know all about these sort of things. Do tell us. Is Paris in France, or France in Paris ? for my wife has been disputing with me about it.' The same gentleman, narrating some conversation which he had heard between the rector and his wife, represented the latter as beginning her reply to her husband with a round oath ; and when his daughter called him to task, reminding him that Mrs. Austen never swore, he replied, ' Now, Betty, why do you pull me up for nothing ? that 's neither here nor there ; you know very well that's only *my way of telling the story.*'

Attention has lately been called by a celebrated
writer to the inferiority of the clergy to the laity of
England two centuries ago. The charge no doubt is
true, if the rural clergy are to be compared with
that higher section of country gentlemen who went
into parliament, and mixed in London society, and
took the lead in their several counties ; but it might
be found less true if they were to be compared, as in
all fairness they ought to be, with that lower section
with whom they usually associated. The smaller
landed proprietors, who seldom went farther from
home than their county town, from the squire with
his thousand acres to the yeoman who cultivated
his hereditary property of one or two hundred, then
formed a numerous class—each the aristocrat of his
own parish ; and there was probably a greater
difference in manners and refinement between this
class and that immediately above them than could
now be found between any two persons who rank as
gentlemen. For in the progress of civilisation,
though all orders may make some progress, yet it is
most perceptible in the lower. It is a process of
' levelling up ; ' the rear rank ' dressing up,' as it
were, close to the front rank. When Hamlet
mentions, as something which he had ' for *three
years taken* note of,' that ' the toe of the peasant
comes so near the heel of the courtier,' it was probably intended by Shakspeare as a satire on his
own times ; but it expressed a principle which is
working at all times in which society makes any

progress. I believe that a century ago the improvement in most country parishes began with the clergy ; and that in those days a rector who chanced to be a gentleman and a scholar found himself superior to his chief parishioners in information and manners, and became a sort of centre of refinement and politeness.

Mr. Austen was a remarkably good-looking man, both in his youth and his old age. During his year of office at Oxford he had been called ' the handsome Proctor ; ' and at Bath, when more than seventy years old, he attracted observation by his fine features and abundance of snow-white hair. Being a good scholar he was able to prepare two of his sons for the University, and to direct the studies of his other children, whether sons or daughters, as well as to increase his income by taking pupils.

In Mrs. Austen also was to be found the germ of much of the ability which was concentrated in Jane, but of which others of her children had a share. She united strong common sense with a lively imagination, and often expressed herself, both in writing and in conversation, with epigrammatic force and point. She lived, like many of her family, to an advanced age. During the last years of her life she endured continual pain, not only patiently but with characteristic cheerfulness. She once said to me, ' Ah, my dear, you find me just where you left me—on the sofa. I sometimes think that God Almighty must have forgotten me ; but I dare say He will come for me in His own good time.' She died and was buried at Chawton, January 1827, aged eighty-eight.

Her own family were so much, and the rest of the world so little, to Jane Austen, that some brief mention of her brothers and sister is necessary in order to give any idea of the objects which principally occupied her thoughts and filled her heart, especially as some of them, from their characters or professions in life, may be supposed to have had more or less influence on her writings : though I feel some reluctance in bringing before public notice persons and circumstances essentially private.

Her eldest brother James, my own father, had, when a very young man, at St. John's College, Oxford, been the originator and chief supporter of a periodical paper called ' The Loiterer,' written somewhat on the plan of the ' Spectator ' and its successors, but nearly confined to subjects connected with the University. In after life he used to speak very slightingly of this early work, which he had the better right to do, as, whatever may have been the degree of their merits, the best papers had certainly been written by himself. He was well read in English literature, had a correct taste, and wrote readily and happily, both in prose and verse. He was more than ten years older than Jane, and had, I believe, a large share in directing her reading and forming her taste.

Her second brother, Edward, had been a good deal separated from the rest of the family, as he was early adopted by his cousin, Mr. Knight, of God-mersham Park in Kent and Chawton House in Hampshire ; and finally came into possession both of the property and the name. But though a good deal separated in childhood, they were much together in after life, and Jane gave a large share of her affections to him and his children. Mr. Knight was not only a very amiable man, kind and indulgent to all connected with him, but possessed also a spirit of fun and liveliness, which made him especially delightful to all young people.

Her third brother, Henry, had great conversational powers, and inherited from his father an eager and sanguine disposition. He was a very entertaining companion, but had perhaps less steadiness of purpose, certainly less success in life, than his brothers. He became a clergyman when middle-aged ; and an allusion to his sermons will be found in one of Jane's letters. At one time he resided in London, and was useful in transacting his sister's business with her publishers.

Her two youngest brothers, Francis and Charles, were sailors during that glorious period of the British navy which comprises the close of the last and the beginning of the present century, when it was impossible for an officer to be almost always afloat, as these brothers were, without seeing service which, in these days, would be considered distinguished. Accordingly, they were continually engaged in actions of more or less importance, and sometimes gained promotion by their success. Both rose to the rank of Admiral, and carried out their flags to distant stations.

Francis lived to attain the very summit of his profession, having died, in his ninety-third year, G.C.B. and Senior Admiral of the Fleet, in 1865. He possessed great firmness of character, with a strong sense of duty, whether due from himself to others, or from others to himself. He was consequently a strict disciplinarian; but, as he was a very religious man, it was remarked of him (for in those days, at least, it was remarkable) that he maintained this discipline without ever uttering an oath or permitting one in his presence. On one occasion, when ashore in a seaside town, he was spoken of as ' *the* officer who kneeled at church ; ' a custom which now happily would not be thought peculiar.

Charles was generally serving in frigates or sloops; blockading harbours, driving the ships of the enemy ashore, boarding gun-boats, and frequently making small prizes. At one time he was absent from England on such services for seven years together. In later life he commanded the Bellerophon, at the bombardment of St. Jean d'Acre in 1840. In 1850 he went out in the Hastings, in command of the East India and China station, but on the breaking out of the Burmese war he transferred his flag to a steam sloop, for the purpose of getting up the shallow waters of the Irrawaddy, on board of which he died of cholera in 1852, in the seventy-fourth year of his age. His sweet temper and affectionate disposition, in which he resembled his sister Jane, had secured to him an unusual portion of attachment, not only from his own family, but from all the officers and common sailors who served under him. One who was with him at his death has left this record of him : ' Our good Admiral won the hearts of all by his gentleness and kindness while he was struggling with disease, and endeavouring to do his duty as Commander-in-chief of the British naval forces in these waters. His death was a great grief to the whole fleet. I know that I cried bitterly when I found he was dead.' The Order in Council of the Governor-General of India, Lord Dalhousie, expresses ' admiration of the staunch high spirit which, notwithstanding his age and previous sufferings, had led the Admiral to take his part in the trying service which has closed his career.'

These two brothers have been dwelt on longer than the others because their honourable career accounts for Jane Austen's partiality for the Navy, as well as for the readiness and accuracy with which she wrote about it. She was always very careful not to meddle with matters which she did not thoroughly understand. She never touched upon politics, law, or medicine, subjects which some novel writers have ventured on rather too boldly, and have treated, perhaps, with more brilliancy than accuracy. But with ships and sailors she felt herself at home, or at least could always trust to a brotherly critic to keep her right. I believe that no flaw has ever been found in her seamanship either in 'Mansfield Park' or in 'Persuasion.'

But dearest of all to the heart of Jane was her sister Cassandra, about three years her senior. Their sisterly affection for each other could scarcely be exceeded. Perhaps it began on Jane's side with the feeling of deference natural to a loving child towards a kind elder sister. Something of this feeling always remained; and even in the maturity of her powers, and in the enjoyment of increasing success, she would still speak of Cassandra as of one wiser and better than herself. In childhood, when the elder was sent to the school of a Mrs. Latournelle, in the Forbury at Reading, the younger went with her, not because she was thought old enough to profit much by the instruction there imparted, but because she would have been miserable without her sister; her mother observing that 'if Cassandra were going to have her head cut off, Jane would insist on sharing her fate.' This attachment was never interrupted or weakened. They lived in the same home, and shared the same bed-room, till separated by death. They were not exactly alike. Cassandra's was the colder and calmer disposition; she was always prudent and well judging, but with less outward demonstration of feeling and less sunniness of temper than Jane possessed. It was remarked in her family that ' Cassandra had the *merit* of having her temper always under command, but that Jane had the *happiness* of a temper that never required to be commanded.' When ' Sense and Sensibility ' came out, some persons, who knew the family slightly, surmised that the two elder Miss Dashwoods were intended by the author for her sister and herself ; but this could not be the case. Cassandra's character might indeed represent the ' *sense* ' of Elinor, but Jane's had little in common with the ' *sensibility* ' of Marianne. The young woman who, before the age of twenty, could so clearly discern the failings of Marianne Dashwood, could hardly have been subject to them herself.

This was the small circle, continually enlarged, however, by the increasing families of four of her brothers, within which Jane Austen found her wholesome pleasures, duties, and interests, and beyond which she went very little into society during the last ten years of her life. There was so much that was agreeable and attractive in this family party that its members may be excused if they were inclined to live somewhat too exclusively within it. They might see in each other much to love and esteem, and something to admire. The family talk had abundance of spirit and vivacity, and was never troubled by disagreements even in little matters, for it was not their habit to dispute or argue with each other : above all, there was strong

family affection and firm union, never to be broken
but by death. It cannot be doubted that all this
had its influence on the author in the construction
of her stories, in which a family party usually
supplies the narrow stage, while the interest is
made to revolve round a few actors.

It will be seen also that though her circle of
society was small, yet she found in her neighbourhood persons of good taste and cultivated minds.
Her acquaintance, in fact, constituted the very class
from which she took her imaginary characters,
ranging from the member of parliament, or large
landed proprietor, to the young curate or younger
midshipman of equally good family; and I think
that the influence of these early associations may
be traced in her writings, especially in two particulars. First, that she is entirely free from the
vulgarity, which is so offensive in some novels, of
dwelling on the outward appendages of wealth or
rank, as if they were things to which the writer was
unaccustomed; and, secondly, that she deals as
little with very low as with very high stations in
life. She does not go lower than the Miss Steeles,
Mrs. Elton, and John Thorpe, people of bad taste
and underbred manners, such as are actually found
sometimes mingling with better society. She has
nothing resembling the Brangtons, or Mr. Dubster
and his friend Tom Hicks, with whom Madame
D'Arblay loved to season her stories, and to produce
striking contrasts to her well bred characters.

CHAPTER II.

As the first twenty-five years, more than half of the brief life of Jane Austen, were spent in the parsonage of Steventon, some description of that place ought to be given. Steventon is a small rural village upon the chalk hills of north Hants, situated in a winding valley about seven miles from Basingstoke. The South-Western railway crosses it by a short embankment, and, as it curves round, presents a good view of it on the left hand to those who are travelling down the line, about three miles before entering the tunnel under Popham Beacon. It may be known to some sportsmen, as lying in one of the best portions of the Vine Hunt. It is certainly not a picturesque country; it presents no grand or extensive views; but the features are small rather than plain. The surface continually swells and sinks, but the hills are not bold, nor the valleys deep; and though it is sufficiently well clothed with woods and hedgerows, yet the poverty of the soil in most places prevents the timber from attaining a large size. Still it has its beauties. The lanes wind along in a natural curve, continually fringed with irregular borders of native turf, and lead to pleasant nooks and corners. One who knew and loved it well very happily expressed its quiet charms, when he wrote

> True taste is not fastidious, nor rejects,
> Because they may not come within the rule
> Of composition pure and picturesque,
> Unnumbered simple scenes which fill the leaves
> Of Nature's sketch book.

Of this somewhat tame country, Steventon, from the fall of the ground, and the abundance of its timber, is certainly one of the prettiest spots ; yet one cannot be surprised that, when Jane's mother, a little before her marriage, was shown the scenery of her future home, she should have thought it un-attractive, compared with the broad river, the rich valley, and the noble hills which she had been accustomed to behold at her native home near Henley-upon-Thames.

The house itself stood in a shallow valley, sur-rounded by sloping meadows, well sprinkled with elm trees, at the end of a small village of cottages, each well provided with a garden, scattered about prettily on either side of the road. It was sufficiently commodious to hold pupils in addition to a growing family, and was in those times considered to be above the average of parsonages ; but the rooms were finished with less elegance than would now be found in the most ordinary dwellings. No cornice marked the junction of wall and ceiling ; while the beams which supported the upper floors projected into the rooms below in all their naked simplicity, covered only by a coat of paint or whitewash : accordingly it has since been considered unworthy of being the Rectory house of a family living, and about forty-five years ago it was pulled down for the purpose of erecting a new house in a far better situation on the opposite side of the valley.

North of the house, the road from Deane to Popham Lane ran at a sufficient distance from the front to allow a carriage drive, through turf and trees. On the south side the ground rose gently, and was occupied by one of those old-fashioned gardens in which vegetables and flowers are combined, flanked and protected on the east by one of the thatched mud walls common in that country, and overshadowed by fine elms. Along the upper or southern side of this garden, ran a terrace of the finest turf, which must have been in the writer's thoughts when she described Catharine Morland's childish delight in ' rolling down the green slope at the back of the house.'

But the chief beauty of Steventon consisted in its hedgerows. A hedgerow, in that country, does not mean a thin formal line of quickset, but an irregular border of copse-wood and timber, often wide enough to contain within it a winding footpath, or a rough cart track. Under its shelter the earliest primroses, anemones, and wild hyacinths were to be found ; sometimes, the first bird's-nest ; and, now and then, the unwelcome adder. Two such hedgerows radiated, as it were, from the parsonage garden. One, a continuation of the turf terrace, proceeded westward, forming the southern boundary of the home meadows ; and was formed into a rustic shrubbery, with occasional seats, entitled ' The Wood Walk.' The other ran straight up the hill, under the name of ' The Church Walk,' because it led to the parish church, as well as to a fine old manor-house, of Henry VIII.'s time, occupied by a family named Digweed, who have for more than a century rented it, together with the chief farm in the parish. The church itself—I speak of it as it then was, before the improvements made by the present rector—

A little spireless fane,
Just seen above the woody lane,

might have appeared mean and uninteresting to an ordinary observer ; but the adept in church archi-tecture would have known that it must have stood there some seven centuries, and would have found beauty in the very narrow early English windows, as well as in the general proportions of its little chancel ; while its solitary position, far from the hum of the village, and within sight of no habitation, except a glimpse of the gray manor-house through its circling screen of sycamores, has in it something solemn and appropriate to the last resting-place of the silent dead. Sweet violets, both purple and white, grow in abundance beneath its south wall.

One may imagine for how many centuries the ancestors of those little flowers have occupied that undisturbed, sunny nook, and may think how few living families can boast of as ancient a tenure of their land. Large elms protrude their rough branches ; old hawthorns shed their annual blossoms over the graves ; and the hollow yew-tree must be at least coeval with the church.

But whatever may be the beauties or defects of the surrounding scenery, this was the residence of Jane Austen for twenty-five years. This was the cradle of her genius. These were the first objects which inspired her young heart with a sense of the beauties of nature. In strolls along those wood-walks, thick-coming fancies rose in her mind, and gradually assumed the forms in which they came forth to the world. In that simple church she brought them all into subjection to the piety which ruled her in life, and supported her in death.

The home at Steventon must have been, for many years, a pleasant and prosperous one. The family was unbroken by death, and seldom visited by sorrow. Their situation had some peculiar advantages beyond those of ordinary rectories. Steventon was a family living. Mr. Knight, the patron, was also proprietor of nearly the whole parish. He never resided there, and consequently the rector and his children came to be regarded in the neighbourhood as a kind of representatives of the family. They shared with the principal tenant the command of an excellent manor, and enjoyed, in this reflected way, some of the consideration usually awarded to landed proprietors. They were not rich, but, aided by Mr. Austen's powers of teaching, they had enough to afford a good education to their sons and daughters, to mix in the best society of the neighbourhood, and to exercise a liberal hospitality to their own relations and friends. A carriage and a pair of horses were kept. This might imply a higher style of living in our days than it did in theirs. There were then no assessed taxes. The carriage, once bought, entailed little further expense; and the horses probably, like Mr. Bennet's, were often employed on farm work. Moreover, it should be remembered that a pair of horses in those days were almost necessary, if ladies were to move about at all; for neither the condition of the roads nor the style of carriage-building admitted of any comfortable vehicle being drawn by a single horse. When one looks at the few specimens still remaining of coach-building in the last century, it strikes one that the chief object of the builders must have been to combine the greatest possible weight with the least possible amount of accommodation.

The family lived in close intimacy with two cousins, Edward and Jane Cooper, the children of Mrs. Austen's eldest sister, and Dr. Cooper, the vicar of Sonning, near Reading. The Coopers lived for some years at Bath, which seems to have been much frequented in those days by clergymen retiring from work. I believe that Cassandra and Jane sometimes visited them there, and that Jane thus acquired the intimate knowledge of the topography and customs of Bath, which enabled her to write ' Northanger Abbey ' long before she resided there herself. After the death of their own parents, the two young Coopers paid long visits at Steventon. Edward Cooper did not live undistinguished. When an undergraduate at Oxford, he gained the prize for Latin hexameters on ' Hortus Anglicus ' in 1791 ; and in later life he was known by a work on prophecy, called ' The Crisis,' and other religious publications, especially for several volumes of Sermons, much preached in many pulpits in my youth. Jane Cooper was married from her uncle's house at Steventon, to Captain, afterwards Sir Thomas Williams, under whom Charles Austen served in several ships. She was a dear friend of her namesake, but was fated to become a cause of great sorrow to her, for a few years after the marriage she was suddenly killed by an accident to her carriage.

There was another cousin closely associated with them at Steventon, who must have introduced greater variety into the family circle. This was the daughter of Mr. Austen's only sister, Mrs. Hancock. This cousin had been educated in Paris, and married to a Count de Feuillade, of whom I know little more than that he perished by the guillotine during the

French Revolution. Perhaps his chief offence was his rank; but it was said that the charge of 'incivism,' under which he suffered, rested on the fact of his having laid down some arable land into pasture—a sure sign of his intention to embarrass the Republican Government by producing a famine! His wife escaped through dangers and difficulties to England, was received for some time into her uncle's family, and finally married her cousin Henry Austen. During the short peace of Amiens, she and her second husband went to France, in the hope of recovering some of the Count's property, and there narrowly escaped being included amongst the *détenus*. Orders had been given by Buonaparte's government to detain all English travellers, but at the post-houses Mrs. Henry Austen gave the necessary orders herself, and her French was so perfect that she passed everywhere for a native, and her husband escaped under this protection.

She was a clever woman, and highly accomplished, after the French rather than the English mode ; and in those days, when intercourse with the Continent was long interrupted by war, such an element in the society of a country parsonage must have been a rare acquisition. The sisters may have been more indebted to this cousin than to Mrs. La Tournelle's teaching for the considerable knowledge of French which they possessed. She also took the principal parts in the private theatricals in which the family several times indulged, having their summer theatre in the barn, and their winter one within the narrow limits of the dining-room, where the number of the audience must have been very limited. On these occasions, the prologues and epilogues were written by Jane's eldest brother, and some of them are very vigorous and amusing. Jane was only twelve years old at the time of the earliest of these representations, and not more than fifteen when the last took place. She was, however, an early observer, and it may be reasonably supposed that some of the incidents and feelings which are so vividly painted in the Mansfield Park theatricals are due to her recollections of these entertainments.

Some time before they left Steventon, one great affliction came upon the family. Cassandra was engaged to be married to a young clergyman. He had not sufficient private fortune to permit an immediate union ; but the engagement was not likely to be a hopeless or a protracted one, for he had a prospect of early preferment from a nobleman with whom he was connected both by birth and by personal friendship. He accompanied this friend to the West Indies, as chaplain to his regiment, and there died of yellow fever, to the great concern of his friend and patron, who afterwards declared that, if he had known of the engagement, he would not have permitted him to go out to such a climate. This little domestic tragedy caused great and lasting grief to the principal sufferer, and could not but cast a gloom over the whole party. The sympathy of

Jane was probably, from her age, and her peculiar attachment to her sister, the deepest of all.

Of Jane herself I know of no such definite tale of love to relate. Her reviewer in the ' Quarterly ' of January 1821 observes, concerning the attachment of Fanny Price to Edmund Bertram : ' The silence in which this passion is cherished, the slender hopes and enjoyments by which it is fed, the restlessness and jealousy with which it fills a mind naturally active, contented, and unsuspicious, the manner in which it tinges every event, and every reflection, are painted with a vividness and a detail of which we can scarcely conceive any one but a female, and we should almost add, a female writing from recollection, capable.' This conjecture, however probable, was wide of the mark. The picture was drawn from the intuitive perceptions of genius, not from personal experience. In no circumstance of her life was there any similarity between herself and her heroine in ' Mansfield Park.' She did not indeed pass through life without being the object of warm affection. In her youth she had declined the addresses of a gentleman who had the recommendations of good character, and connections, and position in life, of everything, in fact, except the subtle power of touching her heart. There is, however, one passage of romance in her history with which I am imperfectly acquainted, and to which I am unable to assign name, or date, or place, though I have it on sufficient authority.

Many years after her death, some circumstances induced her sister Cassandra to break through her habitual reticence, and to speak of it. She said that, while staying at some seaside place, they became acquainted with a gentleman, whose charm of person, mind, and manners was such that Cassandra thought him worthy to possess and likely to win her sister's love. When they parted, he expressed his intention of soon seeing them again ; and Cassandra felt no doubt as to his motives. But they never again met. Within a short time they heard of his sudden death. I believe that, if Jane ever loved, it was this unnamed gentleman ; but the acquaintance had been short, and I am unable to say whether her feelings were of such a nature as to affect her happiness.

Any description that I might attempt of the family life at Steventon, which closed soon after I was born, could be little better than a fancy-piece. There is no doubt that if we could look into the households of the clergy and the small gentry of that period, we should see some things which would seem strange to us, and should miss many more to which we are accustomed. Every hundred years, and especially a century like the last, marked by an extraordinary advance in wealth, luxury, and refinement of taste, as well as in the mechanical arts which embellish our houses, must produce a great change in their aspect. These changes are always at work ; they are going on now, but so silently that we take no

note of them. Men soon forget the small objects
which they leave behind them as they drift down
the stream of life. As Pope says—

> Nor does life's stream for observation stay ;
> It hurries all too fast to mark their way.

Important inventions, such as the applications of
steam, gas, and electricity, may find their places in
history ; but not so the alterations, great as they
may be, which have taken place in the appearance
of our dining and drawing-rooms. Who can now
record the degrees by which the custom prevalent
in my youth of asking each other to take wine
together at dinner became obsolete ? Who will
be able to fix, twenty years hence, the date when
our dinners began to be carved and handed round
by servants, instead of smoking before our eyes and
noses on the table ? To record such little matters
would indeed be ' to chronicle small beer.' But,
in a slight memoir like this, I may be allowed to
note some of those changes in social habits which
give a colour to history, but which the historian
has the greatest difficulty in recovering.

At that time the dinner-table presented a far less
splendid appearance than it does now. It was
appropriated to solid food, rather than to flowers,
fruits, and decorations. Nor was there much glitter
of plate upon it ; for the early dinner hour rendered
candlesticks unnecessary, and silver forks had not
come into general use : while the broad rounded

end of the knives indicated the substitute generally used instead of them.*

The dinners too were more homely, though not less plentiful and savoury ; and the bill of fare in one house would not be so like that in another as it is now, for family receipts were held in high estimation. A grandmother of culinary talent could bequeath to her descendant fame for some particular dish, and might influence the family dinner for many generations.

> Dos est magna parentium
> Virtus.

One house would pride itself on its ham, another on its game-pie, and a third on its superior furmity, or tansey-pudding. Beer and home-made wines, especially mead, were more largely consumed. Vegetables were less plentiful and less various. Potatoes were used, but not so abundantly as now ; and there was an idea that they were to be eaten only with roast meat. They were novelties to a

---

* The celebrated Beau Brummel, who was so intimate with George IV. as to be able to quarrel with him, was born in 1771. It is reported that when he was questioned about his parents, he replied that it was long since he had heard of them, but that he imagined the worthy couple must have cut their own throats by that time, because when he last saw them they were eating peas with their knives. Yet Brummel's father had probably lived in good society ; and was certainly able to put his son into a fashionable regiment, and to leave him 30,000*l.*[1] Raikes believes that he had been Secretary to Lord North. Thackeray's idea that he had been a footman cannot stand against the authority of Raikes, who was intimate with the son.

---

[1] Raikes's *Memoirs*, vol. ii. p. 207.

tenant's wife who was entertained at Steventon
Parsonage, certainly less than a hundred years ago ;
and when Mrs. Austen advised her to plant them
in her own garden, she replied, ' No, no ; they are
very well for you gentry, but they must be terribly
costly to rear.'

But a still greater difference would be found in
the furniture of the rooms, which would appear to
us lamentably scanty. There was a general deficiency of carpeting in sitting-rooms, bed-rooms,
and passages. A pianoforte, or rather a spinnet or
harpsichord, was by no means a necessary appen-
dage. It was to be found only where there was a
decided taste for music, not so common then as now,
or in such great houses as would probably contain
a billiard-table. There would often be but one sofa
in the house, and that a stiff, angular, uncom-
fortable article. There were no deep easy-chairs,
nor other appliances for lounging ; for to lie down,
or even to lean back, was a luxury permitted only
to old persons or invalids. It was said of a nobleman, a personal friend of George III. and a model
gentleman of his day, that he would have made the
tour of Europe without ever touching the back of
his travelling carriage. But perhaps we should be
most struck with the total absence of those elegant
little articles which now embellish and encumber
our drawing-room tables. We should miss the
sliding bookcases and picture-stands, the letter-
weighing machines and envelope cases, the periodi-

cals and illustrated newspapers—above all, the countless swarm of photograph books which now threaten to swallow up all space. A small writing-desk, with a smaller work-box, or netting-case, was all that each young lady contributed to occupy the table; for the large family work-basket, though often produced in the parlour, lived in the closet.

There must have been more dancing throughout the country in those days than there is now : and it seems to have sprung up more spontaneously, as if it were a natural production, with less fastidiousness as to the quality of music, lights, and floor. Many country towns had a monthly ball throughout the winter, in some of which the same apartment served for dancing and tea-room. Dinner parties more frequently ended with an extempore dance on the carpet, to the music of a harpsichord in the house, or a fiddle from the village. This was always supposed to be for the entertainment of the young people, but many, who had little pretension to youth, were very ready to join in it. There can be no doubt that Jane herself enjoyed dancing, for she attributes this taste to her favourite heroines ; in most of her works, a ball or a private dance is mentioned, and made of importance.

Many things connected with the ball-rooms of those days have now passed into oblivion. The barbarous law which confined the lady to one partner throughout the evening must indeed have been abolished before Jane went to balls. It must

be observed, however, that this custom was in one
respect advantageous to the gentleman, inasmuch
as it rendered his duties more practicable.　He was
bound to call upon his partner the next morning,
and it must have been convenient to have only one
lady for whom he was obliged

> To gallop all the country over,
> The last night's partner to behold,
> And humbly hope she caught no cold.

But the stately minuet still reigned supreme ; and
every regular ball commenced with it.　It was a
slow and solemn movement, expressive of grace and
dignity, rather than of merriment.　It abounded in
formal bows and courtesies, with measured paces,
forwards, backwards and sideways, and many com-
plicated gyrations.　It was executed by one lady
and gentleman, amidst the admiration, or the
criticism, of surrounding spectators.　In its earlier
and most palmy days, as when Sir Charles and
Lady Grandison delighted the company by dancing
it at their own wedding, the gentleman wore a dress
sword, and the lady was armed with a fan of nearly
equal dimensions.　Addison observes that ' women
are armed with fans, as men with swords, and sometimes do more execution with them.'　The graceful
carriage of each weapon was considered a test of
high breeding.　The clownish man was in danger of
being tripped up by his sword getting between his
legs : the fan held clumsily looked more of a burden
than an ornament ; while in the hands of an adept

it could be made to speak a language of its own.* It was not everyone who felt qualified to make this public exhibition, and I have been told that those ladies who intended to dance minuets, used to distinguish themselves from others by wearing a particular kind of lappet on their head-dress. I have heard also of another curious proof of the respect in which this dance was held. Gloves immaculately clean were considered requisite for its due performance, while gloves a little soiled were thought good enough for a country dance ; and accordingly some prudent ladies provided themselves with two pairs for their several purposes. The minuet expired with the last century : but long after it had ceased to be danced publicly it was taught to boys and girls, in order to give them a graceful carriage.

Hornpipes, cotillons, and reels, were occasionally danced ; but the chief occupation of the evening was the interminable country dance, in which all could join. This dance presented a great show of enjoyment, but it was not without its peculiar troubles. The ladies and gentlemen were ranged apart from each other in opposite rows, so that the

---

* See 'Spectator,' No. 102, on the Fan Exercise. Old gentlemen who had survived the fashion of wearing swords were known to regret the disuse of that custom, because it put an end to one way of distinguishing those who had, from those who had not, been used to good society. To wear the sword easily was an art which, like swimming and skating, required to be learned in youth. Children could practise it early with their toy swords adapted to their size.

facilities for flirtation, or interesting intercourse, were not so great as might have been desired by both parties. Much heart-burning and discontent sometimes arose as to *who* should stand above *whom*, and especially as to who was entitled to the high privilege of calling and leading off the first dance : and no little indignation was felt at the lower end of the room when any of the leading couples retired prematurely from their duties, and did not condescend to dance up and down the whole set. We may rejoice that these causes of irritation no longer exist ; and that if such feelings as jealousy, rivalry, and discontent ever touch celestial bosoms in the modern ball-room they must arise from different and more recondite sources.

I am tempted to add a little about the difference of personal habits. It may be asserted as a general truth, that less was left to the charge and discretion of servants, and more was done, or superintended, by the masters and mistresses. With regard to the mistresses, it is, I believe, generally understood, that at the time to which I refer, a hundred years ago, they took a personal part in the higher branches of cookery, as well as in the concoction of home-made wines, and distilling of herbs for domestic medicines, which are nearly allied to the same art. Ladies did not disdain to spin the thread of which the household linen was woven. Some ladies liked to wash with their own hands their choice china after breakfast or tea. In one of my earliest child's

books, a little girl, the daughter of a gentleman, is
taught by her mother to make her own bed before
leaving her chamber. It was not so much that they
had not servants to do all these things for them, as
that they took an interest in such occupations.
And it must be borne in mind how many sources of
interest enjoyed by this generation were then
closed, or very scantily opened to ladies. A very
small minority of them cared much for literature
or science. Music was not a very common, and
drawing was a still rarer, accomplishment ; needlework, in some form or other, was their chief seden-
tary employment.

But I doubt whether the rising generation are
equally aware how much gentlemen also did for
themselves in those times, and whether some things
that I can mention will not be a surprise to them.
Two homely proverbs were held in higher estimation in my early days than they are now—' The
master's eye makes the horse fat ; ' and, ' If you
would be well served, serve yourself.' Some gentlemen took pleasure in being their own gardeners,
performing all the scientific, and some of the manual,
work themselves. Well-dressed young men of my
acquaintance, who had their coat from a London
tailor, would always brush their evening suit
themselves, rather than entrust it to the careless-
ness of a rough servant, and to the risks of dirt and
grease in the kitchen ; for in those days servants'
halls were not common in the houses of the clergy

and the smaller country gentry. It was quite
natural that Catherine Morland should have contrasted the magnificence of the offices at Northanger Abbey with the few shapeless pantries in her
father's parsonage. A young man who expected
to have his things packed or unpacked for him by
a servant, when he travelled, would have been
thought exceptionally fine, or exceptionally lazy.
When my uncle undertook to teach me to shoot, his
first lesson was how to clean my own gun. It was
thought meritorious on the evening of a hunting
day, to turn out after dinner, lanthorn in hand, and
visit the stable, to ascertain that the horse had been
well cared for. This was of the more importance,
because, previous to the introduction of clipping,
about the year 1820, it was a difficult and tedious
work to make a long-coated hunter dry and comfortable, and was often very imperfectly done. Of
course, such things were not practised by those
who had gamekeepers, and stud-grooms, and plenty
of well-trained servants ; but they were practised
by many who were unequivocally gentlemen, and
whose grandsons, occupying the same position in
life, may perhaps be astonished at being told that
' *such things were.*'

I have drawn pictures for which my own experience, or what I heard from others in my youth,
have supplied the materials. Of course, they cannot be universally applicable. Such details varied
in various circles, and were changed very gradually;

nor can I pretend to tell how much of what I have said is descriptive of the family life at Steventon in Jane Austen's youth. I am sure that the ladies there had nothing to do with the mysteries of the stew-pot or the preserving-pan ; but it is probable that their way of life differed a little from ours, and would have appeared to us more homely. It may be that useful articles, which would not now be produced in drawing-rooms, were hemmed, and marked, and darned in the old-fashioned parlour. But all this concerned only the outer life ; there was as much cultivation and refinement of mind as now, with probably more studied courtesy and ceremony of manner to visitors ; whilst certainly in that family literary pursuits were not neglected.

I remember to have heard of only two little things different from modern customs. One was, that on hunting mornings the young men usually took their hasty breakfast in the kitchen. The early hour at which hounds then met may account for this ; and probably the custom began, if it did not end, when they were boys ; for they hunted at an early age, in a scrambling sort of way, upon any pony or donkey that they could procure, or, in default of such luxuries, on foot. I have been told that Sir Francis Austen, when seven years old, bought on his own account, it must be supposed with his father's permission, a pony for a guinea and a half ; and after riding him with great success for two seasons, sold him for a guinea more. One may wonder how the child could have so much money, and how the animal could have been obtained for so little. The same authority informs me that his first cloth suit was made from a scarlet habit, which, according to the fashion of the times, had been his mother's usual morning dress. If all this is true, the future admiral of the British Fleet must have cut a conspicuous figure in the hunting-field. The other peculiarity was that, when the roads were dirty, the sisters took long walks in pattens. This defence against wet and dirt is now seldom seen. The few that remain are banished from good society, and employed only in menial work; but a hundred and fifty years ago they were celebrated in poetry, and considered so clever a contrivance that Gay, in his 'Trivia,' ascribes the invention to a god stimulated by his passion for a mortal damsel, and derives the name 'Patten' from 'Patty.'

> The patten now supports each frugal dame,
> Which from the blue-eyed Patty takes the name.

But mortal damsels have long ago discarded the clumsy implement. First it dropped its iron ring and became a clog; afterwards it was fined down into the pliant galoshe—lighter to wear and more effectual to protect—a no less manifest instance of gradual improvement than Cowper indicates when he traces through eighty lines of poetry his 'accomplished sofa' back to the original three-legged stool.

As an illustration of the purposes which a patten was intended to serve, I add the following epigram,

written by Jane Austen's uncle, Mr. Leigh Perrot, on
reading in a newspaper the marriage of Captain
Foote to Miss Patten :—

> Through the rough paths of life, with a patten your guard,
>   May you safely and pleasantly jog ;
> May the knot never slip, nor the ring press too hard,
>   Nor the *Foot* find the *Patten* a clog.

At the time when Jane Austen lived at Steventon,
a work was carried on in the neighbouring cottages
which ought to be recorded, because it has long
ceased to exist.

Up to the beginning of the present century, poor
women found profitable employment in spinning
flax or wool. This was a better occupation for them
than straw plaiting, inasmuch as it was carried on
at the family hearth, and did not admit of gadding
and gossiping about the village. The implement
used was a long narrow machine of wood, raised on
legs, furnished at one end with a large wheel, and at
the other with a spindle on which the flax or wool
was loosely wrapped, connected together by a loop
of string. One hand turned the wheel, while the
other formed the thread. The outstretched arms,
the advanced foot, the sway of the whole figure
backwards and forwards, produced picturesque
attitudes, and displayed whatever of grace or
beauty the work-woman might possess.* Some
ladies were fond of spinning, but they worked in
a quieter manner, sitting at a neat little machine

---

* Mrs. Gaskell, in her tale of ' Sylvia's Lovers,' declares that this
hand-spinning rivalled harp-playing in its gracefulness.

of varnished wood, like Tunbridge ware, generally turned by the foot, with a basin of water at hand to supply the moisture required for forming the thread, which the cottager took by a more direct and natural process from her own mouth. I remember two such elegant little wheels in our own family.

It may be observed that this hand-spinning is the most primitive of female accomplishments, and can be traced back to the earliest times. Ballad poetry and fairy tales are full of allusions to it. The term ' spinster ' still testifies to its having been the ordinary employment of the English young woman. It was the labour assigned to the ejected nuns by the rough earl who said, ' Go spin, ye jades, go spin.' It was the employment at which Roman matrons and Grecian princesses presided amongst their handmaids. Heathen mythology celebrated it in the three Fates spinning and measuring out the thread of human life. Holy Scripture honours it in those ' wise-hearted women ' who ' did spin with their hands, and brought that which they had spun ' for the construction of the Tabernacle in the wilderness : and an old English proverb carries it still farther back to the time ' when Adam delved and Eve span.' But, at last, this time-honoured domestic manufacture is quite extinct amongst us —crushed by the power of steam, overborne by a countless host of spinning jennies, and I can only just remember some of its last struggles for existence in the Steventon cottages.

CHAPTER III.

I know little of Jane Austen's childhood. Her mother followed a custom, not unusual in those days, though it seems strange to us, of putting out her babies to be nursed in a cottage in the village. The infant was daily visited by one or both of its parents, and frequently brought to them at the parsonage, but the cottage was its home, and must have remained so till it was old enough to run about and talk ; for I know that one of them, in after life, used to speak of his foster mother as ' Movie,' the name by which he had called her in his infancy. It may be that the contrast between the parsonage house and the best class of cottages was not quite so extreme then as it would be now, that the one was somewhat less luxurious, and the other less squalid. It would certainly seem from the results that it was a wholesome and invigorating system, for the children were all strong and healthy. Jane was probably treated like the rest in this respect. In childhood every available opportunity of instruction was made use of. According to the ideas of the time, she was well educated, though not highly accomplished, and she certainly enjoyed that important element of mental training, associating at home with persons of cultivated intellect. It cannot be doubted that her early years were bright and happy, living, as she did, with indulgent parents, in a cheerful home, not without agreeable variety of society. To these sources of enjoyment must be added the first stirrings of talent within her, and the absorbing interest of original composition. It is impossible to say at how early an age she began to write. There are copy books extant containing tales some of which must have been composed while she was a young girl, as they had amounted to a considerable number by the time she was sixteen. Her earliest stories are of a slight and flimsy texture, and are generally intended to be nonsensical, but the nonsense has much spirit in it. They are usually preceded by a dedication of mock solemnity to some one of her family. It would seem that the grandiloquent dedications prevalent in those days had not escaped her youthful penetration. Perhaps the most characteristic feature in these early productions is that, however puerile the matter, they are always composed in pure simple English, quite free from the over-ornamented style which might be expected from so young a writer. One of her juvenile effusions is given, as a specimen of the kind of transitory amusement which Jane was continually supplying to the family party.

THE MYSTERY.

AN UNFINISHED COMEDY.

DEDICATION.

To the Rev. George Austen.

Sir,—I humbly solicit your patronage to the following Comedy, which, though an unfinished one, is, I flatter myself, as complete a *Mystery* as any of its kind.

I am, Sir, your most humble Servant,

The Author.

THE MYSTERY, A COMEDY.

DRAMATIS PERSONÆ.

Men.	*Women.*
Col. Elliott.	Fanny Elliott.
Old Humbug.	Mrs. Humbug
Young Humbug.	*and*
Sir Edward Spangle	Daphne.
and	
Corydon.	

ACT I.

Scene I.—*A Garden.*

Enter Corydon.

Corydon. But hush : I am interrupted. [*Exit* Corydon.

Enter Old Humbug *and his* Son, *talking.*

Old Hum. It is for that reason that I wish you to follow my advice. Are you convinced of its propriety ?

Young Hum. I am, sir, and will certainly act in the manner you have pointed out to me.

Old Hum. Then let us return to the house. [*Exeunt.*

SCENE II.—*A parlour in* HUMBUG'S *house.* MRS. HUMBUG
and FANNY *discovered at work.*

Mrs. Hum. You understand me, my love ?

Fanny. Perfectly, ma'am : pray continue your narra-
tion.

Mrs. Hum. Alas ! it is nearly concluded ; for I have
nothing more to say on the subject.

Fanny. Ah ! here is Daphne.

Enter DAPHNE.

Daphne. My dear Mrs. Humbug, how d'ye do ? Oh !
Fanny, it is all over.

Fanny. Is it indeed !

Mrs. Hum. I'm very sorry to hear it.

Fanny. Then 'twas to no purpose that I——

Daphne. None upon earth.

Mrs. Hum. And what is to become of —— ?

Daphne. Oh ! 'tis all settled. (*Whispers* MRS. HUMBUG.)

Fanny. And how is it determined ?

Daphne. I'll tell you. (*Whispers* FANNY.)

Mrs. Hum. And is he to—— ?

Daphne. I'll tell you all I know of the matter. (*Whispers*
MRS. HUMBUG *and* FANNY.)

Fanny. Well, now I know everything about it, I'll go
away.

Mrs. Hum.⎫
Daphne. ⎬And so will I.   [*Exeunt.*

SCENE III.—*The curtain rises, and discovers* SIR EDWARD
SPANGLE *reclined in an elegant attitude on a sofa fast asleep.*

Enter COL. ELLIOTT.

Col. E. My daughter is not here, I see. There lies Sir

Edward. Shall I tell him the secret ? No, he'll certainly blab it. But he's asleep, and won't hear me ;—so I'll e'en venture. (*Goes up to* SIR EDWARD, *whispers him, and exit.*)

END OF THE FIRST ACT.

FINIS.

Her own mature opinion of the desirableness of such an early habit of composition is given in the following words of a niece :—

' As I grew older, my aunt would talk to me more seriously of my reading and my amusements. I had taken early to writing verses and stories, and I am sorry to think how I troubled her with reading them. She was very kind about it, and always had some praise to bestow, but at last she warned me against spending too much time upon them. She said—how well I recollect it !—that she knew writing stories was a great amusement, and *she* thought a harmless one, though many people, she was aware, thought otherwise ; but that at my age it would be bad for me to be much taken up with my own compositions. Later still—it was after she had gone to Winchester —she sent me a message to this effect, that if I would take her advice I should cease writing till I was sixteen ; that she had herself often wished she had read more, and written less in the corresponding years of her own life.' As this niece was only twelve years old at the time of her aunt's death, these words seem to imply that the juvenile tales to which

I have referred had, some of them at least, been written in her childhood.

But between these childish effusions, and the composition of her living works, there intervened another stage of her progress, during which she produced some stories, not without merit, but which she never considered worthy of publication. During this preparatory period her mind seems to have been working in a very different direction from that into which it ultimately settled. Instead of presenting faithful copies of nature, these tales were generally burlesques, ridiculing the improbable events and exaggerated sentiments which she had met with in sundry silly romances. Something of this fancy is to be found in 'Northanger Abbey,' but she soon left it far behind in her subsequent course. It would seem as if she were first taking note of all the faults to be avoided, and curiously considering how she ought *not* to write before she attempted to put forth her strength in the right direction. The family have, rightly, I think, declined to let these early works be published. Mr. Shortreed observed very pithily of Walter Scott's early rambles on the borders, ' He was makin' himsell a' the time ; but he didna ken, may be, what he was about till years had passed. At first he thought of little, I dare say, but the queerness and the fun.' And so, in a humbler way, Jane Austen was ' makin' hersell,' little thinking of future fame, but caring only for ' the queerness and the

fun ; ' and it would be as unfair to expose this pre-
liminary process to the world, as it would be to display all that goes on behind the curtain of the
theatre before it is drawn up.

It was, however, at Steventon that the real
foundations of her fame were laid. There some of
her most successful writing was composéd at such
an early age as to make it surprising that so young
a woman could have acquired the insight into
character, and the nice observation of manners
which they display. 'Pride and Prejudice,' which
some consider the most brilliant of her novels, was
the first finished, if not the first begun. She began
it in October 1796, before she was twenty-one years
old, and completed it in about ten months, in
August 1797. The title then intended for it was
'First Impressions.' 'Sense and Sensibility'
was begun, in its present form, immediately after
the completion of the former, in November 1797 ;
but something similar in story and character had
been written earlier under the title of 'Elinor and
Marianne ; ' and if, as is probable, a good deal of
this earlier production was retained, it must form
the earliest specimen of her writing that has been
given to the world. 'Northanger Abbey,' though
not prepared for the press till 1803, was certainly
first composed in 1798.

Amongst the most valuable neighbours of the
Austens were Mr. and Mrs. Lefroy and their family.
He was rector of the adjoining parish of Ashe ; she

was sister to Sir Egerton Brydges, to whom we are
indebted for the earliest notice of Jane Austen that
exists.　In his autobiography, speaking of his visits
at Ashe, he writes thus : ' The nearest neighbours
of the Lefroys were the Austens of Steventon.　I remember
Jane Austen, the novelist, as a little child.
She was very intimate with Mrs. Lefroy, and much
encouraged by her.　Her mother was a Miss Leigh,
whose paternal grandmother was sister to the first
Duke of Chandos.　Mr. Austen was of a Kentish
family, of which several branches have been settled
in the Weald of Kent, and some are still remaining
there.　When I knew Jane Austen, I never suspected
that she was an authoress ; but my eyes
told me that she was fair and handsome, slight and
elegant, but with cheeks a little too full.'　One may
wish that Sir Egerton had dwelt rather longer on the
subject of these memoirs, instead of being drawn
away by his extreme love for genealogies to her
great-grandmother and ancestors.　That great-grandmother
however lives in the family records as
Mary Brydges, a daughter of Lord Chandos, married
in Westminster Abbey to Theophilus Leigh of
Addlestrop in 1698.　When a girl she had received
a curious letter of advice and reproof, written by
her mother from Constantinople.　Mary, or ' Poll,'
was remaining in England with her grandmother,
Lady Bernard, who seems to have been wealthy and
inclined to be too indulgent to her granddaughter.
This letter is given.　Any such authentic document,

two hundred years old, dealing with domestic details, must possess some interest. This is remarkable, not only as a specimen of the homely language in which ladies of rank then expressed themselves, but from the sound sense which it contains. Forms of expression vary, but good sense and right principles are the same in the nineteenth that they were in the seventeenth century.

' MY DEARES POLL,

' Y^r letters by Cousin Robbert Serle arrived here not before the 27th of Aprill, yett were they hartily wellcome to us, bringing ye joyful news which a great while we had longed for of my most dear Mother & all other relations & friends good health which I beseech God continue to you all, & as I observe in y^{rs} to y^r Sister Betty ye extraordinary kindness of (as I may truly say) the best Moth^r & Gnd Moth^r in the world in pinching herself to make you fine, so I cannot but admire her great good Housewifry in affording you so very plentifull an allowance, & yett to increase her Stock at the rate I find she hath done ; & think I can never sufficiently mind you how very much it is y^r duty on all occasions to pay her y^r gratitude in all humble submission & obedience to all her commands soe long as you live. I must tell you 'tis to her bounty & care in ye greatest measure you are like to owe y^r well living in this world, & as you cannot but be

very sensible you are an extra-ordinary charge to
her so it behoves you to take particular heed th^t in
ye whole course of y^r life, you render her a propor-
tionable comfort, especially since 'tis ye best way
you can ever hope to make her such amends as God
requires of y^r hands. but Poll ! it grieves me a little
& y^t I am forced to take notice of & reprove you for
some vaine expressions in y^r lett^{rs} to y^r Sister—you
say concerning y^r allowance " you aime to bring
y^r bread & cheese even " in this I do not discom-
mend you, for a foule shame indeed it would be
should you out run the Constable having soe
liberall a provision made you for y^r maintenance
—but ye reason you give for y^r resolution I cannot
at all approve for you say " to spend more you
can't " thats because you have it not to spend, otherwise it seems you would. So y^t 'tis y^r Grandmoth^{rs}
discretion & not yours th^t keeps you from extrava-
gancy, which plainly appears in ye close of y^r
sentence, saying y^t you think it simple covetousness
to save out of y^{rs} but 'tis my opinion if you lay all
on y^r back 'tis ten tymes a greater sin & shame th^n
to save some what out of soe large an allowance in
y^r purse to help you at a dead lift. Child, we all
know our beginning, but who knows his end ?
Y^e best use th^t can be made of fair weath^r is to provide against foule & 'tis great discretion & of noe
small commendations for a young woman betymes
to shew herself housewifly & frugal. Y^r Mother
neither Maide nor wife ever yett bestowed forty

pounds a yeare on herself & yett if you never fall
und^r a worse reputation in ye world th^n she (I thank
God for it) hath hitherto done, you need not repine
at it, & you cannot be ignorant of ye difference th^t
was between my fortune & what you are to expect.
You ought likewise to consider th^t you have seven
brothers & sisters & you are all one man's children
& therefore it is very unreasonable that one should
expect to be preferred in finery soe much above all
ye rest for 'tis impossible you should soe much mistake y^r ffather's condition as to fancy he is able to
allow every one of you forty pounds a yeare a piece,
for such an allowance with the charge of their diett
over and above will amount to at least five hundred
pounds a yeare, a sum y^r poor ffather can ill spare,
besides doe but bethink y^{r}self what a ridiculous
sight it will be when y^r grandmoth^r & you come to
us to have noe less th^n seven waiting gentlewomen
in one house, for what reason can you give why
every one of y^r Sist^{rs} should not have every one of
y^m a Maide as well as you, & though you may spare
to pay y^r maide's wages out of y^r allowance yett you
take no care of ye unnecessary charge you put y^r
ffath^r to in y^r increase of his family, whereas if it
were not a piece of pride to have ye name of keeping
y^r maide she y^t waits on y^r good Grandmother
might easily doe as formerly you know she hath
done, all ye business you have for a maide unless as
you grow old^r you grow a veryer Foole which God
forbid !

'Poll, you live in a place where you see great plenty & splendour but let not y[e] allurements of earthly pleasures tempt you to forget or neglect y[e] duty of a good Christian in dressing y[r] bett[r] part which is y[r] soule, as will best please God. I am not against y[r] going decent & neate as becomes y[r] ffathers daughter but to clothe y[r]self rich & be running into every gaudy fashion can never become y[r] circumstances & instead of doing you creditt & getting you a good prefer[nt] it is y[e] readiest way you can take to fright all sober men from ever thinking of matching th[m]selves with women that live above thy[r] fortune, & if this be a wise way of spending money judge you ! & besides, doe but reflect what an od sight it will be to a stranger that comes to our house to see y[r] Grandmoth[r] y[r] Moth[r] & all y[r] Sisters in a plane dress & you only trick[d] up like a bartle-mew-babby—you know what sort of people those are th[t] can't faire well but they must cry rost meate now what effect could you imagine y[r] writing in such a high straine to y[r] Sisters could have but eithe[r] to provoke th[m] to envy you or murmur against us. I must tell you neith[r] of y[r] Sisters have ever had twenty pounds a yeare allowance from us yett, & yett they[r] dress hath not disparaged neith[r] th[m] nor us & without incurring y[e] censure of simple covetousness they will have some what to shew out of their saving that will doe th[m] creditt & I expect y[t] you th[t] are theyr elder Sister sh[d] rather sett th[m] examples of y[e] like nature th[n] tempt th[m] from treading in ye steps of their good Grandmoth^r & poor Moth^r. This is not half what might be saide on this occasion but believing thee to be a very good natured dutyfull child I sh^d have thought it a great deal too much but y^t having in my coming hither past through many most desperate dangers I cannot forbear thinking & preparing myself for all events, & therefore not knowing how it may please God to dispose of us I conclude it my duty to God & thee my d^r child to lay this matter as home to thee as I could, assuring you my daily prayers are not nor shall not be wanting that God may give you grace always to remember to make a right use of this truly affectionate counsell of y^r poor Moth^r. & though I speak very plaine down-right english to you yett I would not have you doubt but that I love you as hartily as any child I have & if you serve God and take good courses I promise you my kindness to you shall be according to y^r own hart's desire, for you may be certain I can aime at nothing in what I have now writ but y^r real good which to promote shall be ye study & care day & night

    ' Of my dear Poll

   ' thy truly affectionate Moth^r.

      ' ELIZA CHANDOS.

' Pera of Galata, May ye 6th 1686.

' P.S.—Thy ffath^r & I send thee our blessing, & all thy broth^rs & sist^rs they^r service. Our harty & affectionate service to my broth^r & sist^r Childe & all

my dear cozens.   When you see my Lady Worster
& cozen Howlands pray present th^m my most
humble service.'

This letter shows that the wealth acquired by
trade was already manifesting itself in contrast with
the straitened circumstances of some of the nobility.
Mary Brydges's ' poor ffather,' in whose household
economy was necessary, was the King of England's
ambassador at Constantinople ; the grandmother,
who lived in ' great plenty and splendour,' was the
widow of a Turkey merchant.   But then, as now,
it would seem, rank had the power of attracting and
absorbing wealth.

At Ashe also Jane became acquainted with a
member of the Lefroy family, who was still living
when I began these memoirs, a few months ago ;
the Right Hon. Thomas Lefroy, late Chief Justice of
Ireland.   One must look back more than seventy
years to reach the time when these two bright young
persons were, for a short time, intimately acquainted
with each other, and then separated on their several
courses, never to meet again ; both destined to
attain some distinction in their different ways, one to
survive the other for more than half a century, yet
in his extreme old age to remember and speak, as he
sometimes did, of his former companion, as one to
be much admired, and not easily forgotten by those
who had ever known her.

Mrs. Lefroy herself was a remarkable person.   Her

rare endowments of goodness, talents, graceful person, and engaging manners, were sufficient to secure her a prominent place in any society into which she was thrown ; while her enthusiastic eagerness of disposition rendered her especially attractive to a clever and lively girl. She was killed by a fall from her horse on Jane's birthday, Dec. 16, 1804. The following lines to her memory were written by Jane four years afterwards, when she was thirty-three years old. They are given, not for their merits as poetry, but to show how deep and lasting was the impression made by the elder friend on the mind of the younger :—

To the Memory of Mrs. Lefroy.

1.

The day returns again, my natal day ;
   What mix'd emotions in my mind arise !
Beloved Friend ; four years have passed away
   Since thou wert snatched for ever from our eyes.

2.

The day commemorative of my birth,
   Bestowing life, and light, and hope to me,
Brings back the hour which was thy last on earth.
   O ! bitter pang of torturing memory !

3.

Angelic woman ! past my power to praise
   In language meet thy talents, temper, mind,
Thy solid worth, thy captivating grace,
   Thou friend and ornament of human kind.

4.

But come, fond Fancy, thou indulgent power ;
   Hope is desponding, chill, severe, to thee :
Bless thou this little portion of an hour ;
   Let me behold her as she used to be.

5.

I see her here with all her smiles benign,
   Her looks of eager love, her accents sweet,
That voice and countenance almost divine,
   Expression, harmony, alike complete.

6.

Listen ! It is not sound alone, 'tis sense,
   'Tis genius, taste, and tenderness of soul :
'Tis genuine warmth of heart without pretence,
   And purity of mind that crowns the whole.

7.

She speaks ! 'Tis eloquence, that grace of tongue,
   So rare, so lovely, never misapplied
By her, to palliate vice, or deck a wrong :
   She speaks and argues but on virtue's side.

8.

Hers is the energy of soul sincere ;
   Her Christian spirit, ignorant to feign,
Seeks but to comfort, heal, enlighten, cheer,
   Confer a pleasure or prevent a pain.

9.

Can aught enhance such goodness ? yes, to me
   Her partial favour from my earliest years
Consummates all : ah ! give me but to see
   Her smile of love ! The vision disappears.

10.

'Tis past and gone. We meet no more below.
  Short is the cheat of Fancy o'er the tomb.
Oh ! might I hope to equal bliss to go,
  To meet thee, angel, in thy future home.

11.

Fain would I feel an union with thy fate :
  Fain would I seek to draw an omen fair
From this connection in our earthly date.
  Indulge the harmless weakness. Reason, spare.

The loss of their first home is generally a great
grief to young persons of strong feeling and lively
imagination ; and Jane was exceedingly unhappy
when she was told that her father, now seventy
years of age, had determined to resign his duties to
his eldest son, who was to be his successor in the
Rectory of Steventon, and to remove with his wife
and daughters to Bath. Jane had been absent from
home when this resolution was taken ; and, as her
father was always rapid both in forming his resolu-
tions and in acting on them, she had little time to
reconcile herself to the change.

A wish has sometimes been expressed that some
of Jane Austen's letters should be published. Some
entire letters, and many extracts, will be given in
this memoir ; but the reader must be warned not to
expect too much from them. With regard to
accuracy of language indeed every word of them
might be printed without correction. The style

is always clear, and generally animated, while a
vein of humour continually gleams through the
whole ; but the materials may be thought inferior
to the execution, for they treat only of the details
of domestic life. There is in them no notice of
politics or public events ; scarcely any discussions
on literature, or other subjects of general interest.
They may be said to resemble the nest which some
little bird builds of the materials nearest at hand, of
the twigs and mosses supplied by the tree in which
it is placed ; curiously constructed out of the
simplest matters.

Her letters have very seldom the date of the year,
or the signature of her christian name at full length ;
but it has been easy to ascertain their dates, either
from the post-mark, or from their contents.

The two following letters are the earliest that I
have seen. They were both written in November
1800 ; before the family removed from Steventon.
Some of the same circumstances are referred to in
both.

The first is to her sister Cassandra, who was then
staying with their brother Edward at Godmersham
Park, Kent :—

'Steventon, Saturday evening, Nov. 8th.

My dear Cassandra,

'I thank you for so speedy a return to my two
last, and particularly thank you for your anecdote of

Charlotte Graham and her cousin, Harriet Bailey, which has very much amused both my mother and myself. If you can learn anything farther of that interesting affair, I hope you will mention it. I have two messages ; let me get rid of them, and then my paper will be my own. Mary fully intended writing to you by Mr. Chute's frank, and only happened entirely to forget it, but will write soon ; and my father wishes Edward to send him a memorandum of the price of the hops. The tables are come, and give general contentment. I had not expected that they would so perfectly suit the fancy of us all three, or that we should so well agree in the disposition of them ; but nothing except their own surface can have been smoother. The two ends put together form one constant table for everything, and the centre piece stands exceedingly well under the glass, and holds a great deal most commodiously, without looking awkwardly. They are both covered with green baize, and send their best love. The Pembroke has got its destination by the sideboard, and my mother has great delight in keeping her money and papers locked up. The little table which used to stand there has most conveniently taken itself off into the best bedroom ; and we are now in want only of the chiffonniere, which is neither finished nor come. So much for that subject ; I now come to another, of a very different nature, as other subjects are very apt to be. Earle Harwood has been again giving uneasiness to his family and talk to the neighbourhood ; in the present instance, however, he is only unfortunate, and not in fault.

' About ten days ago, in cocking a pistol in the guard-room at Marcau, he accidentally shot himself through the thigh. Two young Scotch surgeons in the island were polite enough to propose taking off the thigh at once, but to that he would not consent ; and accordingly in his wounded state was put on board a cutter and conveyed to Haslar Hospital, at Gosport, where the bullet was extracted, and where he now is, I hope, in a fair way of doing well. The surgeon of the hospital wrote to the family on the occasion, and John Harwood went down to him immediately, attended by James,* whose object in going was to be the means of bringing back the earliest intelligence to Mr. and Mrs. Harwood, whose anxious sufferings, particularly those of the latter, have of course been dreadful. They went down on Tuesday, and James came back the next day, bringing such favourable accounts as greatly to lessen the distress of the family at Deane, though it will probably be a long while before Mrs. Harwood can be quite at ease. *One* most material comfort, however, they have ; the assurance of its being really an accidental wound, which is not only positively declared by Earle himself, but is likewise testified by the particular direction of the bullet. Such a wound could not have been received in a duel. At present he is going on very well, but

* James, the writer's eldest brother.

the surgeon will not declare him to be in no danger.*
Mr. Heathcote met with a genteel little accident the
other day in hunting. He got off to lead his horse
over a hedge, or a house, or something, and his horse
in his haste trod upon his leg, or rather ancle, I
believe, and it is not certain whether the small bone
is not broke. Martha has accepted Mary's invitation for Lord Portsmouth's ball. He has not yet
sent out his own invitations, but *that* does not
signify ; Martha comes, and a ball there is to be.
I think it will be too early in her mother's absence
for me to return with her.

' *Sunday Evening*.—We have had a dreadful
storm of wind in the fore part of this day, which has
done a great deal of mischief among our trees. I
was sitting alone in the dining-room when an odd
kind of crash startled me—in a moment afterwards
it was repeated. I then went to the window, which
I reached just in time to see the last of our two
highly valued elms descend into the Sweep ! ! ! ! !
The other, which had fallen, I suppose, in the first
crash, and which was the nearest to the pond,
taking a more easterly direction, sunk among our
screen of chestnuts and firs, knocking down one
spruce-fir, beating off the head of another, and
stripping the two corner chestnuts of several
branches in its fall. This is not all. One large
elm out of the two on the left-hand side as you
enter what I call the elm walk, was likewise blown

* The limb was saved.

down ; the maple bearing the weathercock was broke in two, and what I regret more than all the rest is, that all the three elms which grew in Hall's meadow, and gave such ornament to it, are gone ; two were blown down, and the other so much injured that it cannot stand. I am happy to add, however, that no greater evil than the loss of trees has been the consequence of the storm in this place, or in our immediate neighbourhood. We grieve, therefore, in some comfort.

' I am yours ever,   ' J. A.'

The next letter, written four days later than the former, was addressed to Miss Lloyd, an intimate friend, whose sister (my mother) was married to Jane's eldest brother :—

'Steventon, Wednesday evening, Nov. 12th.

' MY DEAR MARTHA,

' I did not receive your note yesterday till after Charlotte had left Deane, or I would have sent my answer by her, instead of being the means, as I now must be, of lessening the elegance of your new dress for the Hurstbourne ball by the value of 3*d.* You are very good in wishing to see me at Ibthorp so soon, and I am equally good in wishing to come to you. I believe our merit in that respect is much upon a par, our self-denial mutually strong. Having paid this tribute of praise to the virtue of both, I shall here have done with panegyric, and proceed to plain matter of fact. In about a fortnight's time I hope to be with you. I have two reasons for not being able to come before. I wish so to arrange my visit as to spend some days with you after your mother's return. In the 1st place, that I may have the pleasure of seeing her, and in the 2nd, that I may have a better chance of bringing you back with me. Your promise in my favour was not quite absolute, but if your will is not perverse, you and I will do all in our power to overcome your scruples of conscience. I hope we shall meet next week to talk all this over, till we have tired ourselves with the very idea of my visit before my visit begins. Our invitations for the 19th are arrived, and very curiously are they worded.* Mary mentioned to you yesterday poor Earle's unfortunate accident, I dare say. He does not seem to be going on very well. The two or three last posts have brought less and less favourable accounts of him. John Harwood has gone to Gosport again to-day. We have two families of friends now who are in a most anxious state ; for though by a note from Catherine this morning there seems now to be a revival of hope at Manydown, its continuance may

* The invitation, the ball dress, and some other things in this and the preceding letter refer to a ball annually given at Hurstbourne Park, on the anniversary of the Earl of Portsmouth's marriage with his first wife. He was the Lord Portsmouth whose eccentricities afterwards became notorious, and the invitations, as well as other arrangements about these balls, were of a peculiar character.

be too reasonably doubted. Mr. Heathcote,* however, who has broken the small bone of his leg, is so
good as to be going on very well. It would be really
too much to have three people to care for.

' You distress me cruelly by your request about
books. I cannot think of any to bring with me, nor
have I any idea of our wanting them. I come to
you to be talked to, not to read or hear reading ; I
can do that at home ; and indeed I am now laying
in a stock of intelligence to pour out on you as my
share of the conversation. I am reading Henry's
History of England, which I will repeat to you in
any manner you may prefer, either in a loose,
desultory, unconnected stream, or dividing my
recital, as the historian divides it himself, into
seven parts :—The Civil and Military : Religion :
Constitution : Learning and Learned Men : Arts
and Sciences : Commerce, Coins, and Shipping :
and Manners. So that for every evening in the
week there will be a different subject. The Friday's
lot—Commerce, Coins, and Shipping—you will find
the least entertaining ; but the next evening's
portion will make amends. With such a provision
on my part, if you will do yours by repeating the
French Grammar, and Mrs. Stent † will now and
then ejaculate some wonder about the cocks and

* The father of Sir William Heathcote, of Hursley, who was married
to a daughter of Mr. Bigg Wither, of Manydown, and lived in the
neighbourhood.

† A very dull old lady, then residing with Mrs. Lloyd.

hens, what can we want ? Farewell for a short time. We all unite in best love, and I am your very affectionate

'J. A.'

The two next letters must have been written early in 1801, after the removal from Steventon had been decided on, but before it had taken place. They refer to the two brothers who were at sea, and give some idea of a kind of anxieties and uncertainties to which sisters are seldom subject in these days of peace, steamers, and electric telegraphs. At that time ships were often windbound or becalmed, or driven wide of their destination ; and sometimes they had orders to alter their course for some secret service ; not to mention the chance of conflict with a vessel of superior power—no improbable occurrence before the battle of Trafalgar. Information about relatives on board men-of-war was scarce and scanty, and often picked up by hearsay or chance means ; and every scrap of intelligence was proportionably valuable :—

' MY DEAR CASSANDRA,

' I should not have thought it necessary to write to you so soon, but for the arrival of a letter from Charles to myself. It was written last Saturday from off the Start, and conveyed to Popham Lane by Captain Boyle, on his way to Midgham. He came from Lisbon in the " Endymion." I will copy

Charles's account of his conjectures about Frank : " He has not seen my brother lately, nor does he expect to find him arrived, as he met Captain Inglis at Rhodes, going up to take command of the ' Petrel,' as he was coming down ; but supposes he will arrive in less than a fortnight from this time, in some ship which is expected to reach England about that time with dispatches from Sir Ralph Abercrombie." The event must show what sort of a conjuror Captain Boyle is. The " Endymion " has not been plagued with any more prizes. Charles spent three pleasant days in Lisbon.

' They were very well satisfied with their royal passenger,* whom they found jolly and affable, who talks of Lady Augusta as his wife, and seems much attached to her.

' When this letter was written, the " Endymion " was becalmed, but Charles hoped to reach Portsmouth by Monday or Tuesday. He received my letter, communicating our plans, before he left England ; was much surprised, of course, but is quite reconciled to them, and means to come to Steventon once more while Steventon is ours.'

From a letter written later in the same year :—

' Charles has received 30*l*. for his share of the privateer, and expects 10*l*. more ; but of what avail is it to take prizes if he lays out the produce in

* The Duke of Sussex, son of George III., married, without royal consent, to the Lady Augusta Murray.

presents to his sisters ? He has been buying gold chains and topaze crosses for us. He must be well scolded. The " Endymion " has already received orders for taking troops to Egypt, which I should not like at all if I did not trust to Charles being removed from her somehow or other before she sails. He knows nothing of his own destination, he says, but desires me to write directly, as the " Endymion " will probably sail in three or four days. He will receive my yesterday's letter, and I shall write again by this post to thank and reproach him. We shall be unbearably fine.'

CHAPTER IV.

Removal from Steventon—Residences at Bath and at Southampton—
Settling at Chawton.

THE family removed to Bath in the spring of 1801,
where they resided first at No. 4 Sydney Terrace,
and afterwards in Green Park Buildings. I do not
know whether they were at all attracted to Bath by
the circumstance that Mrs. Austen's only brother,
Mr. Leigh Perrot, spent part of every year there.
The name of Perrot, together with a small estate at
Northleigh in Oxfordshire, had been bequeathed to
him by a great uncle. I must devote a few sentences
to this very old and now extinct branch of the
Perrot family ; for one of the last survivors, Jane
Perrot, married to a Walker, was Jane Austen's
great grandmother, from whom she derived her
Christian name. The Perrots were settled in
Pembrokeshire at least as early as the thirteenth
century. They were probably some of the settlers
whom the policy of our Plantagenet kings placed in
that county, which thence acquired the name of
' England beyond Wales,' for the double purpose of
keeping open a communication with Ireland from
Milford Haven, and of overawing the Welsh. One
of the family seems to have carried out this latter

purpose very vigorously ; for it is recorded of him that he slew *twenty-six men* of Kemaes, a district of Wales, and *one wolf.* The manner in which the two kinds of game are classed together, and the disproportion of numbers, are remarkable ; but probably at that time the wolves had been so closely killed down, that *lupicide* was become a more rare and distinguished exploit than *homicide.* The last of this family died about 1778, and their property was divided between Leighs and Musgraves, the larger portion going to the latter. Mr. Leigh Perrot pulled down the mansion, and sold the estate to the Duke of Marlborough, and the name of these Perrots is now to be found only on some monuments in the church of Northleigh.

Mr. Leigh Perrot was also one of several cousins to whom a life interest in the Stoneleigh property in Warwickshire was left, after the extinction of the earlier Leigh peerage, but he compromised his claim to the succession in his lifetime. He married a niece of Sir Montague Cholmeley of Lincolnshire. He was a man of considerable natural power, with much of the wit of his uncle, the Master of Balliol, and wrote clever epigrams and riddles, some of which, though without his name, found their way into print ; but he lived a very retired life, dividing his time between Bath and his place in Berkshire called Scarlets. Jane's letters from Bath make frequent mention of this uncle and aunt.

The unfinished story, now published under the

title of ' The Watsons,' must have been written during the author's residence in Bath. In the autumn of 1804 she spent some weeks at Lyme, and became acquainted with the Cobb, which she afterwards made memorable for the fall of Louisa Musgrove. In February 1805, her father died at Bath, and was buried at Walcot Church. The widow and daughters went into lodgings for a few months, and then removed to Southampton. The only records that I can find about her during those four years are the three following letters to her sister ; one from Lyme, the others from Bath. They shew that she went a good deal into society, in a quiet way, chiefly with ladies ; and that her eyes were always open to minute traits of character in those with whom she associated :—

Extract from a letter from Jane Austen to her Sister.

' Lyme, Friday, Sept. 14 (1804).

' MY DEAR CASSANDRA,—I take the first sheet of fine striped paper to thank you for your letter from Weymouth, and express my hopes of your being at Ibthorp before this time. I expect to hear that you reached it yesterday evening, being able to get as far as Blandford on Wednesday. Your account of Weymouth contains nothing which strikes me so forcibly as there being no ice in the town. For every other vexation I was in some measure prepared, and particularly for your disappointment in not seeing the Royal Family go on board on Tuesday, having already heard from Mr. Crawford that he had seen you in the very act of being too late. But for there being no ice, what could prepare me ! You found my letter at Andover, I hope, yesterday, and have now for many hours been satisfied that your kind anxiety on my behalf was as much thrown away as kind anxiety usually is. I continue quite well; in proof of which I have bathed again this morning. It was absolutely necessary that I should have the little fever and indisposition which I had : it has been all the fashion this week in Lyme. We are quite settled in our lodgings by this time, as you may suppose, and everything goes on in the usual order. The servants behave very well, and make no diffi-culties, though nothing certainly can exceed the inconvenience of the offices, except the general dirtiness of the house and furniture, and all its in-habitants. I endeavour, as far as I can, to supply your place, and be useful, and keep things in order. I detect dirt in the water decanters, as fast as I can, and keep everything as it was under your adminis-tration. . . . The ball last night was pleasant, but not full for Thursday. My father staid contentedly till half-past nine (we went a little after eight), and then walked home with James and a lanthorn, though I believe the lanthorn was not lit, as the moon was up ; but sometimes this lanthorn may be a great convenience to him. My mother and I staid about an hour later. Nobody asked me the two first dances ; the two next I danced with Mr. Crawford, and had I chosen to stay longer might have danced with Mr. Granville, Mrs. Granville's son, whom my dear friend Miss A. introduced to me, or with a new odd-looking man who had been eyeing me for some time, and at last, without any introduction, asked me if I meant to dance again. I think he must be Irish by his ease, and because I imagine him to belong to the hon^{bl} B.'s, who are son, and son's wife of an Irish viscount, bold queer-looking people, just fit to be quality at Lyme. I called yesterday morning (ought it not in strict propriety to be termed yester-morning?) on Miss A. and was introduced to her father and mother. Like other young ladies she is considerably genteeler than her parents. Mrs. A. sat darning a pair of stockings the whole of my visit. But do not mention this at home, lest a warning should act as an example. We afterwards walked together for an hour on the Cobb ; she is very converseable in a common way ; I do not perceive wit or genius, but she has sense and some degree of taste, and her manners are very engaging. She seems to like people rather too easily.

' Your's affect^{ly},

' J. A.'

Letter from Jane Austen to her sister Cassandra at Ibthorp, alluding to the sudden death of Mrs. Lloyd at that place :—

'25 Gay Street (Bath), Monday,
'April 8, 1805.

'MY DEAR CASSANDRA,—Here is a day for you.
Did Bath or Ibthorp ever see such an 8th of April ?
It is March and April together ; the glare of the one
and the warmth of the other. We do nothing but
walk about. As far as your means will admit, I
hope you profit by such weather too. I dare say
you are already the better for change of place. We
were out again last night. Miss Irvine invited us,
when I met her in the Crescent, to drink tea with
them, but I rather declined it, having no idea that
my mother would be disposed for another evening
visit there so soon ; but when I gave her the
message, I found her very well inclined to go ; and
accordingly, on leaving Chapel, we walked to Lans-
down. This morning we have been to see Miss
Chamberlaine look hot on horseback. Seven years
and four months ago we went to the same riding-
house to see Miss Lefroy's performance ! * What
a different set are we now moving in ! But seven
years, I suppose, are enough to change every pore
of one's skin and every feeling of one's mind. We
did not walk long in the Crescent yesterday. It
was hot and not crowded enough ; so we went into
the field, and passed close by S. T. and Miss S.†
again. I have not yet seen her face, but neither her
dress nor air have anything of the dash or stylish-

* Here is evidence that Jane Austen was acquainted with Bath
before it became her residence in 1801. See p. [25].

† A gentleman and lady lately engaged to be married.

ness which the Browns talked of ; quite the contrary ; indeed, her dress is not even smart, and her
appearance very quiet. Miss Irvine says she is
never speaking a word. Poor wretch ; I am afraid
she is *en pénitence.* Here has been that excellent
Mrs. Coulthart calling, while my mother was out,
and I was believed to be so. I always respected her,
as a good-hearted friendly woman. And the
Browns have been here ; I find their affidavits on
the table. The " Ambuscade " reached Gibraltar
on the 9th of March, and found all well ; so say the
papers. We have had no letters from anybody, but
we expect to hear from Edward to-morrow, and
from you soon afterwards. How happy they are at
Godmersham now ! I shall be very glad of a letter
from Ibthorp, that I may know how you all are,
but particularly yourself. This is nice weather for
Mrs. J. Austen's going to Speen, and I hope she will
have a pleasant visit there. I expect a prodigious
account of the christening dinner ; perhaps it
brought you at last into the company of Miss
Dundas again.

' *Tuesday.*—I received your letter last night, and
wish it may be soon followed by another to say that
all is over ; but I cannot help thinking that nature
will struggle again, and produce a revival. Poor
woman ! May her end be peaceful and easy as the
exit we have witnessed ! And I dare say it will. If
there is no revival, suffering must be all over ; even
the consciousness of existence, I suppose, was gone

when you wrote. The nonsense I have been writing
in this and in my last letter seems out of place at
such a time, but I will not mind it ; it will do you no
harm, and nobody else will be attacked by it. I am
heartily glad that you can speak so comfortably of
your own health and looks, though I can scarcely
comprehend the latter being really approved.
Could travelling fifty miles produce such an immediate change ? You were looking very poorly
here, and everybody seemed sensible of it. Is there
a charm in a hack postchaise ? But if there were,
Mrs. Craven's carriage might have undone it all.
I am much obliged to you for the time and trouble
you have bestowed on Mary's cap, and am glad it
pleases her ; but it will prove a useless gift at
present, I suppose. Will not she leave Ibthorp on
her mother's death ? As a companion you are all
that Martha can be supposed to want, and in that
light, under these circumstances, your visit will
indeed have been well timed.

' *Thursday.*—I was not able to go on yesterday ;
all my wit and leisure were bestowed on letters to
Charles and Henry. To the former I wrote in consequence of my mother's having seen in the papers
that the " Urania " was waiting at Portsmouth for
the convoy for Halifax. This is nice, as it is only
three weeks ago that you wrote by the " Camilla."
I wrote to Henry because I had a letter from him in
which he desired to hear from me very soon. His to
me was most affectionate and kind, as well as enter-

taining ; there is no merit to him in *that* ; he cannot
help being amusing. He offers to meet us on the
sea coast, if the plan of which Edward gave him
some hint takes place. Will not this be making
the execution of such a plan more desirable and
delightful than ever ? He talks of the rambles we
took together last summer with pleasing affection.

' Yours ever,

' J. A.'

From the same to the same.

' Gay St. Sunday Evening,
' April 21 (1805).

' MY DEAR CASSANDRA,—I am much obliged to
you for writing to me again so soon ; your letter
yesterday was quite an unexpected pleasure. Poor
Mrs. Stent ! it has been her lot to be always in the
way ; but we must be merciful, for perhaps in time
we may come to be Mrs. Stents ourselves, unequal
to anything, and unwelcome to everybody. . . . My
morning engagement was with the Cookes, and our
party consisted of George and Mary, a Mr. L., Miss
B., who had been with us at the concert, and the
youngest Miss W. Not Julia ; we have done with
her ; she is very ill ; but Mary. Mary W.'s turn is
actually come to be grown up, and have a fine complexion, and wear great square muslin shawls. I
have not expressly enumerated myself among the
party, but there I was, and my cousin George was
very kind, and talked sense to me every now and

then, in the intervals of his more animated fooleries
with Miss B., who is very young, and rather handsome, and whose gracious manners, ready wit, and
solid remarks, put me somewhat in mind of my old
acquaintance L. L.   There was a monstrous deal
of stupid quizzing and common-place nonsense
talked, but scarcely any wit ; all that bordered on
it or on sense came from my cousin George, whom
altogether I like very well.   Mr. B. seems nothing
more than a tall young man.   My evening engagement and walk was with Miss A., who had called
on me the day before, and gently upbraided me in
her turn with a change of manners to her since she
had been in Bath, or at least of late.   Unlucky me !
that my notice should be of such consequence, and
my manners so bad ! She was so well disposed, and
so reasonable, that I soon forgave her, and made
this engagement with her in proof of it.   She is
really an agreeable girl, so I think I may like
her ; and her great want of a companion at home,
which may well make any tolerable acquaintance
important to her, gives her another claim on my
attention.   I shall endeavour as much as possible
to keep my intimacies in their proper place, and
prevent their clashing.   Among so many friends, it
will be well if I do not get into a scrape ; and now
here is Miss Blashford come.   I should have gone
distracted if the Bullers had staid. . . . When I tell
you I have been visiting a countess this morning,
you will immediately, with great justice, but no

truth, guess it to be Lady Roden. No : it is Lady
Leven, the mother of Lord Balgonie. On receiving
a message from Lord and Lady Leven through the
Mackays, declaring their intention of waiting on us,
we thought it right to go to them. I hope we have
not done too much, but the friends and admirers of
Charles must be attended to. They seem very
reasonable, good sort of people, very civil, and full
of his praise.* We were shewn at first into an
empty drawing-room, and presently in came his
lordship, not knowing who we were, to apologise
for the servant's mistake, and to say himself what
was untrue, that Lady Leven was not within. He
is a tall gentlemanlike looking man, with spectacles,
and rather deaf. After sitting with him ten minutes
we walked away ; but Lady Leven coming out of
the dining parlour as we passed the door, we were
obliged to attend her back to it, and pay our visit
over again. She is a stout woman, with a very
handsome face. By this means we had the pleasure
of hearing Charles's praises twice over. They think
themselves excessively obliged to him, and estimate
him so highly as to wish Lord Balgonie, when he is
quite recovered, to go out to him. There is a pretty
little Lady Marianne of the party, to be shaken
hands with, and asked if she remembered Mr.
Austen. . . .

   * It seems that Charles Austen, then first lieutenant of the ' Endymion,' had had an opportunity of shewing attention and kindness to
some of Lord Leven's family.

' I shall write to Charles by the next packet, unless you tell me in the meantime of your intending to do it.

' Believe me, if you chuse,
' Y^r aff^te Sister.'

Jane did not estimate too highly the ' Cousin George ' mentioned in the foregoing letter ; who might easily have been superior in sense and wit to the rest of the party. He was the Rev. George Leigh Cooke, long known and respected at Oxford, where he held important offices, and had the privilege of helping to form the minds of men more eminent than himself. As Tutor in Corpus Christi College, he became instructor to some of the most distinguished undergraduates of that time : amongst others to Dr. Arnold, the Rev. John Keble, and Sir John Coleridge. The latter has mentioned him in terms of affectionate regard, both in his Memoir of Keble, and in a letter which appears in Dean Stanley's ' Life of Arnold.' Mr. Cooke was also an impressive preacher of earnest awakening sermons. I remember to have heard it observed by some of my undergraduate friends that, after all, there was more good to be got from George Cooke's plain sermons than from much of the more laboured oratory of the University pulpit. He was frequently Examiner in the schools, and occupied the chair of the Sedleian Professor of Natural Philosophy, from 1810 to 1853.

.Before the end of 1805, the little family party
removed to Southampton. They resided in a commodious old-fashioned house in a corner of Castle
Square.

I have no letters of my aunt, nor any other record
of her, during her four years' residence at Southampton ; and though I now began to know, and, what
was the same thing, to love her myself, yet my
observations were only those of a young boy, and
were not capable of penetrating her character, or
estimating her powers. I have, however, a lively
recollection of some local circumstances at Southampton, and as they refer chiefly to things which
have been long ago swept away, I will record them.
My grandmother's house had a pleasant garden,
bounded on one side by the old city walls ; the top
of this wall was sufficiently wide to afford a pleasant
walk, with an extensive view, easily accessible to
ladies by steps. This must have been a part of the
identical walls which witnessed the embarkation
of Henry V. before the battle of Agincourt, and
the detection of the conspiracy of Cambridge,
Scroop, and Grey, which Shakspeare has made so
picturesque ; when, according to the chorus in
Henry V., the citizens saw

> The well-appointed King at Hampton Pier
> Embark his royalty.

Among the records of the town of Southampton,
they have a minute and authentic account, drawn

up at that time, of the encampment of Henry V.
near the town, before his embarkment for France.
It is remarkable that the place where the army was
encamped, then a low level plain, is now entirely
covered by the sea, and is called Westport.* At
that time Castle Square was occupied by a fantastic
edifice, too large for the space in which it stood,
though too small to accord well with its castellated
style, erected by the second Marquis of Lansdowne,
half-brother to the well-known statesman, who
succeeded him in the title. The Marchioness had
a light phaeton, drawn by six, and sometimes by
eight little ponies, each pair decreasing in size, and
becoming lighter in colour, through all the grades of
dark brown, light brown, bay, and chestnut, as it
was placed farther away from the carriage. The
two leading pairs were managed by two boyish
postilions, the two pairs nearest to the carriage
were driven in hand. It was a delight to me to
look down from the window and see this fairy equi-
page put together ; for the premises of this castle
were so contracted that the whole process went on
in the little space that remained of the open square.
Like other fairy works, however, it all proved
evanescent. Not only carriage and ponies, but
castle itself, soon vanished away, ' like the baseless
fabric of a vision.' On the death of the Marquis in
1809, the castle was pulled down. Few probably
remember its existence ; and any one who might

* See Wharton's note to Johnson and Steevens' Shakspeare.

visit the place now would wonder how it ever could have stood there.

In 1809 Mr. Knight was able to offer his mother the choice of two houses on his property ; one near his usual residence at Godmersham Park in Kent ; the other near Chawton House, his occasional residence in Hampshire. The latter was chosen ; and in that year the mother and daughters, together with Miss Lloyd, a near connection who lived with them, settled themselves at Chawton Cottage.

Chawton may be called the *second*, as well as the *last* home of Jane Austen ; for during the temporary residences of the party at Bath and Southampton she was only a sojourner in a strange land ; but here she found a real home amongst her own people. It so happened that during her residence at Chawton circumstances brought several of her brothers and their families within easy distance of the house. Chawton must also be considered the place most closely connected with her career as a writer ; for there it was that, in the maturity of her mind, she either wrote or rearranged, and prepared for publication the books by which she has become known to the world. This was the home where, after a few years, while still in the prime of life, she began to droop and wither away, and which she left only in the last stage of her illness, yielding to the persuasion of friends hoping against hope.

This house stood in the village of Chawton, about a mile from Alton, on the right hand side, just where the road to Winchester branches off from that to Gosport. It was so close to the road that the front door opened upon it ; while a very narrow enclosure, paled in on each side, protected the building from danger of collision with any runaway vehicle. I believe it had been originally built for an inn, for which purpose it was certainly well situated. Afterwards it had been occupied by Mr. Knight's steward; but by some additions to the house, and some judicious planting and skreening, it was made a pleasant and commodious abode. Mr. Knight was experienced and adroit at such arrangements, and this was a labour of love to him. A good-sized entrance and two sitting-rooms made the length of the house, all intended originally to look upon the road, but the large drawing-room window was blocked up and turned into a book-case, and another opened at the side which gave to view only turf and trees, as a high wooden fence and hornbeam hedge shut out the Winchester road, which skirted the whole length of the little domain. Trees were planted each side to form a shrubbery walk, carried round the enclosure, which gave a sufficient space for ladies' exercise. There was a pleasant irregular mixture of hedgerow, and gravel walk, and orchard, and long grass for mowing, arising from two or three little enclosures having been thrown together. The house itself was quite as good as the generality of parsonage-houses then were, and much in the same style ; and was capable of receiving other members of the family as frequent visitors. It was sufficiently well furnished ; everything inside and out was kept in good repair, and it was altogether a comfortable and ladylike establishment, though the means which supported it were not large.

I give this description because some interest is generally taken in the residence of a popular writer. Cowper's unattractive house in the street of Olney has been pointed out to visitors, and has even attained the honour of an engraving in Southey's edition of his works : but I cannot recommend any admirer of Jane Austen to undertake a pilgrimage to this spot. The building indeed still stands, but it has lost all that gave it its character. After the death of Mrs. Cassandra Austen, in 1845, it was divided into tenements for labourers, and the grounds reverted to ordinary uses.

CHAPTER V.

Description of Jane Austen's person, character, and tastes.

As my memoir has now reached the period when I saw a great deal of my aunt, and was old enough to understand something of her value, I will here attempt a description of her person, mind, and habits. In person she was very attractive ; her figure was rather tall and slender, her step light and firm, and her whole appearance expressive of health and animation. In complexion she was a clear brunette with a rich colour ; she had full round cheeks, with mouth and nose small and well formed, bright hazel eyes, and brown hair forming natural curls close round her face. If not so regularly handsome as her sister, yet her countenance had a peculiar charm of its own to the eyes of most beholders. At the time of which I am now writing, she never was seen, either morning or evening, without a cap ; I believe that she and her sister were generally thought to have taken to the garb of middle age earlier than their years or their looks required ; and that, though remarkably neat in their dress as in all their ways, they were scarcely sufficiently regardful of the fashionable, or the becoming.

She was not highly accomplished according to the present standard. Her sister drew well, and it is from a drawing of hers that the likeness prefixed to this volume has been taken. Jane herself was fond of music, and had a sweet voice, both in singing and in conversation ; in her youth she had received some instruction on the pianoforte ; and at Chawton she practised daily, chiefly before breakfast. I believe she did so partly that she might not disturb the rest of the party who were less fond of music. In the evening she would sometimes sing, to her own accompaniment, some simple old songs, the words and airs of which, now never heard, still linger in my memory.

She read French with facility, and knew something of Italian. In those days German was no more thought of than Hindostanee, as part of a lady's education. In history she followed the old guides—Goldsmith, Hume, and Robertson. Critical enquiry into the usually received statements of the old historians was scarcely begun. The history of the early kings of Rome had not yet been dissolved into legend. Historic characters lay before the reader's eyes in broad light or shade, not much broken up by details. The virtues of King Henry VIII. were yet undiscovered, nor had much light been thrown on the inconsistencies of Queen Elizabeth ; the one was held to be an unmitigated tyrant, and an embodied Blue Beard ; the other a perfect model of wisdom and policy. Jane, when a girl, had strong political opinions, especially about the affairs of the sixteenth and seventeenth centuries. She was a vehement defender of Charles I. and his grandmother Mary ; but I think it was rather from an impulse of feeling than from any enquiry into the evidences by which they must be condemned or acquitted. As she grew up, the politics of the day occupied very little of her attention, but she probably shared the feeling of moderate Toryism which prevailed in her family. She was well acquainted with the old periodicals from the ' Spectator ' downwards. Her knowledge of Richardson's works was such as no one is likely again to acquire, now that the multitude and the merits of our light literature have called off the attention of readers from that great master. Every circumstance narrated in Sir Charles Grandison, all that was ever said or done in the cedar parlour, was familiar to her ; and the wedding days of Lady L. and Lady G. were as well remembered as if they had been living friends. Amongst her favourite writers, Johnson in prose, Crabbe in verse, and Cowper in both, stood high. It is well that the native good taste of herself and of those with whom she lived, saved her from the snare into which a sister novelist had fallen, of imitating the grandiloquent style of Johnson. She thoroughly enjoyed Crabbe ; perhaps on account of a certain resemblance to herself in minute and highly finished detail ; and would sometimes say, in jest, that, if she ever married at all, she could fancy being Mrs. Crabbe ; looking on the author quite as an abstract idea, and ignorant and regardless what manner of man he might be. Scott's poetry gave her great pleasure ; she did not live to make much acquaintance with his novels. Only three of them were published before her death ; but it will be seen by the following extract from one of her letters, that she was quite prepared to admit the merits of ' Waverley ' ; and it is remarkable that, living, as she did, far apart from the gossip of the literary world, she should even then have spoken so confidently of his being the author of it :—

' Walter Scott has no business to write novels ; especially good ones. It is not fair. He has fame and profit enough as a poet, and ought not to be taking the bread out of other people's mouths. I do not mean to like " Waverley," if I can help it, but I fear I must. I am quite determined, however, not to be pleased with Mrs.——'s, should I ever meet with it, which I hope I may not. I think I can be stout against anything written by her. I have made up my mind to like no novels really, but Miss Edgeworth's, E.'s, and my own.'

It was not, however, what she *knew*, but what she *was*, that distinguished her from others. I cannot better describe the fascination which she exercised over children than by quoting the words of two of her nieces. One says :—

' As a very little girl I was always creeping up to aunt Jane, and following her whenever I could, in the house and out of it. I might not have remembered this but for the recollection of my mother's

telling me privately, that I must not be troublesome to my aunt. Her first charm to children was
great sweetness of manner. She seemed to love you,
and you loved her in return. This, as well as I can
now recollect, was what I felt in my early days,
before I was old enough to be amused by her clever-
ness. But soon came the delight of her playful talk.
She could make everything amusing to a child.
Then, as I got older, when cousins came to share the
entertainment, she would tell us the most delightful stories, chiefly of Fairyland, and her fairies had
all characters of their own. The tale was invented,
I am sure, at the moment, and was continued for
two or three days, if occasion served.'

Again : ' When staying at Chawton, with two of
her other nieces, we often had amusements in which
my aunt was very helpful. She was the one to
whom we always looked for help. She would
furnish us with what we wanted from her wardrobe ;
and she would be the entertaining visitor in our
make-believe house. She amused us in various
ways. Once, I remember, in giving a conversation
as between myself and my two cousins, supposing
we were all grown up, the day after a ball.'

Very similar is the testimony of another niece :—
' Aunt Jane was the general favourite with children ;
her ways with them being so playful, and her long
circumstantial stories so delightful. These were
continued from time to time, and were begged for on
all possible and impossible occasions ; woven, as

she proceeded, out of nothing but her own happy talent for invention. Ah ! if but one of them could be recovered ! And again, as I grew older, when the original seventeen years between our ages seemed to shrink to seven, or to nothing, it comes back to me now how strangely I missed her. It had become so much a habit with me to put by things in my mind with a reference to her, and to say to myself, I shall keep this for aunt Jane.'

A nephew of hers used to observe that his visits to Chawton, after the death of his aunt Jane, were always a disappointment to him. From old associations he could not help expecting to be particularly happy in that house ; and never till he got there could he realise to himself how all its peculiar charm was gone. It was not only that the chief light in the house was quenched, but that the loss of it had cast a shade over the spirits of the survivors. Enough has been said to show her love for children, and her wonderful power of entertaining them ; but her friends of all ages felt her enlivening influence. Her unusually quick sense of the ridiculous led her to play with all the common-places of everyday life, whether as regarded persons or things ; but she never played with its serious duties or responsibilities, nor did she ever turn individuals into ridicule. With all her neighbours in the village she was on friendly, though not on intimate, terms. She took a kindly interest in all their proceedings, and liked to hear about them. They often served for her amusement ; but it was her own nonsense that gave zest to the gossip. She was as far as possible from being censorious or satirical. She never abused them or *quizzed* them—*that* was the word of the day; an ugly word, now obsolete ; and the ugly practice which it expressed is much less prevalent now than it was then. The laugh which she occasionally raised was by imagining for her neighbours, as she was equally ready to imagine for her friends or herself, impossible contingencies, or by relating in prose or verse some trifling anecdote coloured to her own fancy, or in writing a fictitious history of what they were supposed to have said or done, which could deceive nobody.

The following specimens may be given of the liveliness of mind which imparted an agreeable flavour both to her correspondence and her conversation :—

ON READING IN THE NEWSPAPERS THE MARRIAGE OF MR. GELL TO MISS GILL, OF EASTBOURNE.

At Eastbourne Mr. Gell, From being perfectly well,
Became dreadfully ill, For love of Miss Gill.
So he said, with some sighs, I'm the slave of your *iis* ;
Oh, restore, if you please, By accepting my *ees*.

ON THE MARRIAGE OF A MIDDLE-AGED FLIRT WITH A MR. WAKE, WHOM, IT WAS SUPPOSED. SHE WOULD SCARCELY HAVE ACCEPTED IN HER YOUTH.

Maria, good-humoured, and handsome, and tall,
    For a husband was at her last stake ;
And having in vain danced at many a ball,
    Is now happy to *jump at a Wake*.

' We were all at the play last night to see Miss O'Neil in Isabella. I do not think she was quite equal to my expectation. I fancy I want something more than can be. Acting seldom satisfies me. I took two pockethandkerchiefs, but had very little occasion for either. She is an elegant creature, however, and hugs Mr. Young delightfully.'

' So, Miss B. is actually married, but I have never seen it in the papers ; and one may as well be single if the wedding is not to be in print.'

Once, too, she took it into her head to write the following mock panegyric on a young friend, who really was clever and handsome :—

I.

In measured verse I'll now rehearse
  The charms of lovely Anna :
And, first, her mind is unconfined
  Like any vast savannah.

2.

Ontario's lake may fitly speak
  Her fancy's ample bound :
Its circuit may, on strict survey
  Five hundred miles be found.

3.

Her wit descends on foes and friends
  Like famed Niagara's Fall ;
And travellers gaze in wild amaze,
  And listen, one and all.

4.

Her judgment sound, thick, black, profound,
    Like transatlantic groves,
Dispenses aid, and friendly shade
    To all that in it roves.

5.

If thus her mind to be defined
    America exhausts,
And all that's grand in that great land
    In similes it costs—

6.

Oh how can I her person try
    To image and portray ?
How paint the face, the form how trace
    In which those virtues lay ?

7.

Another world must be unfurled,
    Another language known,
Ere tongue or sound can publish round
    Her charms of flesh and bone.

I believe that all this nonsense was nearly extempore, and that the fancy of drawing the images from America arose at the moment from the obvious rhyme which presented itself in the first stanza.

The following extracts are from letters addressed to a niece who was at that time amusing herself by attempting a novel, probably never finished, certainly never published, and of which I know nothing but what these extracts tell. They show the good-natured sympathy and encouragement which the aunt, then herself occupied in writing ' Emma,' could give to the less matured powers of the niece. They bring out incidentally some of her opinions concerning compositions of that kind :—

Extracts.

'Chawton, Aug. 10, 1814.

' Your aunt C. does not like desultory novels, and is rather fearful that yours will be too much so ; that there will be too frequent a change from one set of people to another, and that circumstances will be sometimes introduced, of apparent consequence, which will lead to nothing. It will not be so great an objection to me. I allow much more latitude than she does, and think nature and spirit cover many sins of a wandering story. And people in general do not care much about it, for your comfort. . . .'

'Sept. 9.

' You are now collecting your people delightfully, getting them exactly into such a spot as is the delight of my life. Three or four families in a country village is the very thing to work on ; and I hope you will write a great deal more, and make full use of them while they are so very favourably arranged.'

'Sept. 28.

' Devereux Forrester being ruined by his vanity is very good : but I wish you would not let him plunge into a " vortex of dissipation." I do not object to the thing, but I cannot bear the expression : it is such thorough novel slang ; and so old that I dare say Adam met with it in the first novel that he opened.'

'Hans Place (Nov. 1814).

' I have been very far from finding your book an evil, I assure you. I read it immediately, and with great pleasure. Indeed, I do think you get on very fast. I wish other people of my acquaintance could compose as rapidly. Julian's history was quite a surprise to me. You had not very long known it yourself, I suspect ; but I have no objection to make to the circumstance ; it is very well told, and his having been in love with the aunt gives Cecilia an additional interest with him. I like the idea ; a very proper compliment to an aunt ! I rather imagine, indeed, that nieces are seldom chosen but in compliment to some aunt or other. I dare say your husband was in love with me once, and would never have thought of you if he had not supposed me dead of a scarlet fever.'

Jane Austen was successful in everything that she attempted with her fingers. None of us could throw spilikins in so perfect a circle, or take them off with so steady a hand. Her performances with cup and ball were marvellous. The one used at Chawton was an easy one, and she has been known to catch it on the point above an hundred times in succession, till her hand was weary. She sometimes found a resource in that simple game, when unable, from weakness in her eyes, to read or write long together. A specimen of her clear strong handwriting is here given. Happy would the compositors for the press be if they had always so legible a manuscript to work from. But the writing was not the only part of her letters which showed superior handiwork. In those days there was an art in folding and sealing. No adhesive envelopes made all easy. Some people's letters always looked loose and untidy ; but her paper was sure to take the right folds, and her sealing-wax to drop into the right place. Her needlework both plain and ornamental was excellent, and might almost have put a sewing machine to shame. She was considered especially great in satin stitch. She spent much time in these occupations, and some of her merriest talk was over clothes which she and her companions were making, sometimes for themselves, and sometimes for the poor. There still remains a curious specimen of her needlework made for a sister-in-law, my mother. In a very small bag is deposited a little rolled up housewife, furnished with minikin needles and fine thread. In the housewife is a tiny pocket, and in the pocket is enclosed a slip of paper, on which, written as with a crow quill, are these lines :—

This little bag, I hope, will prove
   To be not vainly made ;
For should you thread and needles want,
   It will afford you aid.

And, as we are about to part,
   'T will serve another end :
For, when you look upon this bag,
   You'll recollect your friend.

It is the kind of article that some benevolent fairy might be supposed to give as a reward to a diligent little girl. The whole is of flowered silk, and having been never used and carefully preserved, it is as fresh and bright as when it was first made seventy years ago ; and shows that the same hand which painted so exquisitely with the pen could work as delicately with the needle.

I have collected some of the bright qualities which shone, as it were, on the surface of Jane Austen's character, and attracted most notice ; but underneath them there lay the strong foundations of sound sense and judgment, rectitude of principle, and delicacy of feeling, qualifying her equally to advise, assist, or amuse. She was, in fact, as ready to comfort the unhappy, or to nurse the sick, as she was to laugh and jest with the light-hearted. Two of her nieces were grown up, and one of them was married, before she was taken away from them. As their minds became more matured, they were admitted into closer intimacy with her,

and learned more of her graver thoughts ; they
know what a sympathising friend and judicious
adviser they found her to be in many little diffi-
culties and doubts of early womanhood.

I do not venture to speak of her religious principles : that is a subject on which she herself was
more inclined to *think* and *act* than to *talk*, and I
shall imitate her reserve ; satisfied to have shown
how much of Christian love and humility abounded
in her heart, without presuming to lay bare the roots
whence those graces grew. Some little insight, however, into these deeper recesses of the heart must
be given, when we come to speak of her death.

CHAPTER VI.

*Habits of Composition resumed after a long interval—First publication—
The interest taken by the Author in the success of her Works.*

IT may seem extraordinary that Jane Austen
should have written so little during the years that
elapsed between leaving Steventon and settling at
Chawton ; especially when this cessation from work
is contrasted with her literary activity both before
and after that period. It might rather have been
expected that fresh scenes and new acquaintance
would have called forth her powers ; while the
quiet life which the family led both at Bath and
Southampton must have afforded abundant leisure
for composition ; but so it was that nothing which
I know of, certainly nothing which the public have
seen, was completed in either of those places. I can
only state the fact, without assigning any cause for
it ; but as soon as she was fixed in her second home,
she resumed the habits of composition which had
been formed in her first, and continued them to
the end of her life. The first year of her residence
at Chawton seems to have been devoted to revising
and preparing for the press ' Sense and Sensibility,'
and ' Pride and Prejudice ' ; but between February
1811 and August 1816, she began and completed
' Mansfield Park,' ' Emma,' and ' Persuasion,' so

that the last five years of her life produced the same number of novels with those which had been written in her early youth. How she was able to effect all this is surprising, for she had no separate study to retire to, and most of the work must have been done in the general sitting-room, subject to all kinds of casual interruptions. She was careful that her occupation should not be suspected by servants, or visitors, or any persons beyond her own family party. She wrote upon small sheets of paper which could easily be put away, or covered with a piece of blotting paper. There was, between the front door and the offices, a swing door which creaked when it was opened ; but she objected to having this little inconvenience remedied, because it gave her notice when anyone was coming. She was not, however, troubled with companions like her own Mrs. Allen in ' Northanger Abbey,' whose ' vacancy of mind and incapacity for thinking were such that, as she never talked a great deal, so she could never be entirely silent ; and therefore, while she sat at work, if she lost her needle, or broke her thread, or saw a speck of dirt on her gown, she must observe it, whether there were any one at leisure to answer her or not.' In that well occupied female party there must have been many precious hours of silence during which the pen was busy at the little mahogany writing-desk,* while Fanny Price, or

* This mahogany desk, which has done good service to the public, is now in the possession of my sister, Miss Austen.

Emma Woodhouse, or Anne Elliott was growing
into beauty and interest. I have no doubt that I,
and my sisters and cousins, in our visits to Chawton,
frequently disturbed this mystic process, without
having any idea of the mischief that we were
doing; certainly we never should have guessed
it by any signs of impatience or irritability in the
writer.

As so much had been previously prepared, when
once she began to publish, her works came out
in quick succession. 'Sense and Sensibility'
was published in 1811, 'Pride and Prejudice'
at the beginning of 1813, 'Mansfield Park'
in 1814, 'Emma' early in 1816; 'Northanger
Abbey' and 'Persuasion' did not appear till
after her death, in 1818. It will be shown farther
on why 'Northanger Abbey,' though amongst the
first written, was one of the last published. Her
first three novels were published by Egerton, her
last three by Murray. The profits of the four
which had been printed before her death had
not at that time amounted to seven hundred
pounds.

I have no record of the publication of 'Sense and
Sensibility,' nor of the author's feelings at this
her first appearance before the public; but the
following extracts from three letters to her sister
give a lively picture of the interest with which she
watched the reception of 'Pride and Prejudice,'
and show the carefulness with which she corrected

her compositions, and rejected much that had been written :—

'I hope you received my little parcel by J. Bond on Wednesday evening, my dear Cassandra, and that you will be ready to hear from me again on Sunday, for I feel that I must write to you to-day. I want to tell you that I have got my own darling child from London. On Wednesday I received one copy sent down by Falkener, with three lines from Henry to say that he had given another to Charles and sent a third by the coach to Godmersham. . . . The advertisement is in our paper to-day for the first time : 18*s.* He shall ask 1*l.* 1*s.* for my two next, and 1*l.* 8*s.* for my stupidest of all. Miss B. dined with us on the very day of the book's coming, and in the evening we fairly set at it, and read half the first vol. to her, prefacing that, having intelligence from Henry that such a work would soon appear, we had desired him to send it whenever it came out, and I believe it passed with her unsuspected. She was amused, poor soul ! *That* she could not help, you know, with two such people to lead the way, but she really does seem to admire Elizabeth. I must confess that I think her as delightful a creature as ever appeared in print, and how I shall be able to tolerate those who do not like *her* at least I do not know. There are a few typical errors ; and a " said he," or a " said she," would sometimes make the dialogue more immediately clear ; but " I do not write for such dull elves " as have not a great deal of ingenuity themselves. The second volume is shorter than I could wish, but the difference is not so much in reality as in look, there being a larger proportion of narrative in that part. I have lop't and crop't so successfully, however, that I imagine it must be rather shorter than " Sense and Sensibility " altogether. Now I will try and write of something else.'

'Chawton, Thursday, February 4 (1813).

' My DEAR CASSANDRA,—Your letter was truly welcome, and I am much obliged to you for all your praise ; it came at a right time, for I had had some fits of disgust. Our second evening's reading to Miss B. had not pleased me so well, but I believe something must be attributed to my mother's too rapid way of getting on : though she perfectly understands the characters herself, she cannot speak as they ought. Upon the whole, however, I am quite vain enough and well satisfied enough. The work is rather too light, and bright, and sparkling ; it wants shade ; it wants to be stretched out here and there with a long chapter of sense, if it could be had ; if not, of solemn specious nonsense, about something unconnected with the story ; an essay on writing, a critique on Walter Scott, or the history of Buonaparté, or something that would form a contrast, and bring the reader with increased delight to the playfulness and epigrammatism of

the general style. . . . The greatest blunder in the
printing that I have met with is in page 220, v. 3,
where two speeches are made into one. There
might as well be no suppers at Longbourn ; but
I suppose it was the remains of Mrs. Bennett's old
Meryton habits.'

The following letter seems to have been written
soon after the last two : in February 1813 :—

' This will be a quick return for yours, my dear
Cassandra ; I doubt its having much else to recommend it ; but there is no saying ; it may turn out to
be a very long and delightful letter. I am exceedingly pleased that you can say what you do, after
having gone through the whole work, and Fanny's
praise is very gratifying. My hopes were tolerably
strong of *her*, but nothing like a certainty. Her
liking Darcy and Elizabeth is enough. She might
hate all the others, if she would. I have her opinion
under her own hand this morning, but your trans-
cript of it, which I read first, was not, and is not, the
less acceptable. To *me* it is of course all praise, but
the more exact truth which she sends *you* is good
enough. . . . Our party on Wednesday was not
unagreeable, though we wanted a master of the
house less anxious and fidgety, and more conver-
sible. Upon Mrs. ——'s mentioning that she had
sent the rejected addresses to Mrs. H., I began
talking to her a little about them, and expressed
my hope of their having amused her. Her answer

was, " Oh dear yes, very much, very droll indeed,
the opening of the house, and the striking up of the
fiddles ! " What she meant, poor woman, who shall
say ? I sought no farther. As soon as a whist party
was formed, and a round table threatened, I made
my mother an excuse and came away, leaving just
as many for *their* round table as there were at Mrs.
Grant's.* I wish they might be as agreeable a set.
My mother is very well, and finds great amusement
in glove-knitting, and at present wants no other
work. We quite run over with books. She has got
Sir John Carr's " Travels in Spain," and I am
reading a Society octavo, an " Essay on the Military
Police and Institutions of the British Empire," by
Capt. Pasley of the Engineers, a book which I protested against at first, but which upon trial I find
delightfully written and highly entertaining. I am
as much in love with the author as I ever was with
Clarkson or Buchanan, or even the two Mr. Smiths
of the city. The first soldier I ever sighed for ; but
he does write with extraordinary force and spirit.
Yesterday, moreover, brought us " Mrs. Grant's
Letters," with Mr. White's compliments ; but I
have disposed of them, compliments and all, to
Miss P., and amongst so many readers or retainers
of books as we have in Chawton, I dare say there
will be no difficulty in getting rid of them for
another fortnight, if necessary. I have disposed of
Mrs. Grant for the second fortnight to Mrs. ——.

* At this time, February 1813, ' Mansfield Park ' was nearly finished.

It can make no difference to *her* which of the twenty-six fortnights in the year the 3 vols. lie on her table. I have been applied to for information as to the oath taken in former times of Bell, Book, and Candle, but have none to give. Perhaps you may be able to learn something of its origin where you now are. Ladies who read those enormous great stupid thick quarto volumes which one always sees in the break-fast parlour there must be acquainted with every-thing in the world. I detest a quarto. Capt. Pasley's book is too good for their society. They will not understand a man who condenses his thoughts into an octavo. I have learned from Sir J. Carr that there is no Government House at Gibraltar. I must alter it to the Commissioner's.'

The following letter belongs to the same year, but treats of a different subject. It describes a journey from Chawton to London, in her brother's curricle, and shows how much could be seen and enjoyed in course of a long summer's day by leisurely travel-ling amongst scenery which the traveller in an express train now rushes through in little more than an hour, but scarcely sees at all :—

'Sloane Street, Thursday, May 20 (1813).

'MY DEAR CASSANDRA,

'Before I say anything else, I claim a paper full of halfpence on the drawing-room mantel-piece ; I put them there myself, and forgot to bring them

with me. I cannot say that I have yet been in any
distress for money, but I chuse to have my due, as
well as the Devil. How lucky we were in our
weather yesterday ! This wet morning makes one
more sensible of it. We had no rain of any consequence. The head of the curricle was put half
up three or four times, but our share of the showers
was very trifling, though they seemed to be heavy
all round us, when we were on the Hog's-back, and
I fancied it might then be raining so hard at Chawton as to make you feel for us much more than we
deserved. Three hours and a quarter took us to
Guildford, where we staid barely two hours, and
had only just time enough for all we had to do
there ; that is, eating a long and comfortable breakfast, watching the carriages, paying Mr. Harrington,
and taking a little stroll afterwards. From some
views which that stroll gave us, I think most highly
of the situation of Guildford. We wanted all our
brothers and sisters to be standing with us in the
bowling-green, and looking towards Horsham. I
was very lucky in my gloves—got them at the first
shop I went to, though I went into it rather because
it was near than because it looked at all like a glove
shop, and gave only four shillings for them ; after
which everybody at Chawton will be hoping and
predicting that they cannot be good for anything,
and their worth certainly remains to be proved ;
but I think they look very well. We left Guildford
at twenty minutes before twelve (I hope somebody

cares for these minutiæ), and were at Esher in about
two hours more. I was very much pleased with
the country in general. Between Guildford and
Ripley I thought it particularly pretty, also about
Painshill ; and from a Mr. Spicer's grounds at
Esher, which we walked into before dinner, the
views were beautiful. I cannot say what we did
not see, but I should think there could not be a
wood, or a meadow, or palace, or remarkable spot in
England that was not spread out before us on one
side or other. Claremont is going to be sold : a Mr.
Ellis has it now. It is a house that seems never to
have prospered. After dinner we walked forward to
be overtaken at the coachman's time, and before
he did overtake us we were very near Kingston. I
fancy it was about half-past six when we reached
this house—a twelve hours' business, and the
horses did not appear more than reasonably tired.
I was very tired too, and glad to get to bed early,
but am quite well to-day. I am very snug in the
front drawing-room all to myself, and would not
say " thank you " for any company but you. The
quietness of it does me good. I have contrived to
pay my two visits, though the weather made me
a great while about it, and left me only a few
minutes to sit with Charlotte Craven.* She looks
very well, and her hair is done up with an elegance
to do credit to any education. Her manners are as

* The present Lady Pollen, of Redenham, near Andover, then at a
school in London.

unaffected and pleasing as ever. She had heard from her mother to-day. Mrs. Craven spends another fortnight at Chilton. I saw nobody but Charlotte, which pleased me best. I was shewn upstairs into a drawing-room, where she came to me, and the appearance of the room, so totally unschool-like, amused me very much; it was full of modern elegancies.

'Yours very affec^{tly.},   'J. A.'

The next letter, written in the following year, contains an account of another journey to London, with her brother Henry, and reading with him the manuscript of 'Mansfield Park':—

'Henrietta Street, Wednesday, March 2 (1814).

'MY DEAR CASSANDRA,

'You were wrong in thinking of us at Guildford last night: we were at Cobham. On reaching G. we found that John and the horses were gone on. We therefore did no more than we had done at Farnham—sit in the carriage while fresh horses were put in, and proceeded directly to Cobham, which we reached by seven, and about eight were sitting down to a very nice roast fowl, &c. We had altogether a very good journey, and everything at Cobham was comfortable. I could not pay Mr. Harrington! That was the only alas! of the business. I shall therefore return his bill, and my mother's 2*l.*, that you may try your luck. We did

not begin reading till Bentley Green. Henry's
approbation is hitherto even equal to my wishes.
He says it is different from the other two, but does
not appear to think it at all inferior. He has only
married Mrs. R. I am afraid he has gone through
the most entertaining part. He took to Lady B.
and Mrs. N. most kindly, and gives great praise to
the drawing of the characters. He understands
them all, likes Fanny, and, I think, foresees how
it will all be. I finished the " Heroine " last night,
and was very much amused by it. I wonder James
did not like it better. It diverted me exceedingly.
We went to bed at ten. I was very tired, but slept
to a miracle, and am lovely to-day, and at present
Henry seems to have no complaint. We left
Cobham at half-past eight, stopped to bait and
breakfast at Kingston, and were in this house considerably before two. Nice smiling Mr. Barlowe
met us at the door and, in reply to enquiries after
news, said that peace was generally expected.
I have taken possession of my bedroom, unpacked
my bandbox, sent Miss P.'s two letters to the two-
penny post, been visited by M^{d.} B., and am now
writing by myself at the new table in the front
room. It is snowing. We had some snowstorms
yesterday, and a smart frost at night, which
gave us a hard road from Cobham to Kingston ;
but as it was then getting dirty and heavy, Henry
had a pair of leaders put on to the bottom of Sloane
St. His own horses, therefore, cannot have had

hard work. I watched for *veils* as we drove through the streets, and had the pleasure of seeing several upon vulgar heads. And now, how do you all do ? —you in particular, after the worry of yesterday and the day before. I hope Martha had a pleasant visit again, and that you and my mother could eat your beef-pudding. Depend upon my thinking of the chimney-sweeper as soon as I wake to-morrow. Places are secured at Drury Lane for Saturday, but so great is the rage for seeing Kean that only a third and fourth row could be got ; as it is in a front box, however, I hope we shall do pretty well—Shylock, a good play for Fanny—she cannot be much affected, I think. Mrs. Perigord has just been here. She tells me that we owe her master for the silk-dyeing. My poor old muslin has never been dyed yet. It has been promised to be done several times. What wicked people dyers are. They begin with dipping their own souls in scarlet sin. It is evening. We have drank tea, and I have torn through the third vol. of the " Heroine." I do not think it falls off. It is a delightful burlesque, particularly on the Radcliffe style. Henry is going on with " Mansfield Park." He admires H. Crawford : I mean properly, as a clever, pleasant man. I tell you all the good I can, as I know how much you will enjoy it. We hear that Mr. Kean is more admired than ever. There are no good places to be got in Drury Lane for the next fortnight, but Henry means to secure some for Saturday fortnight, when

you are reckoned upon.   Give my love to little Cass.
I hope she found my bed comfortable last night.
I have seen nobody in London yet with such a long
chin as Dr. Syntax, nor anybody quite so large as
Gogmagolicus.

' Yours aff^{ly}.,

' J. AUSTEN.'

CHAPTER VII.

JANE AUSTEN lived in entire seclusion from the literary world : neither by correspondence, nor by personal intercourse was she known to any contemporary authors. It is probable that she never was in company with any person whose talents or whose celebrity equalled her own ; so that her powers never could have been sharpened by collision with superior intellects, nor her imagination aided by their casual suggestions. Whatever she produced was a genuine home-made article. Even during the last two or three years of her life, when her works were rising in the estimation of the public, they did not enlarge the circle of her acquaintance. Few of her readers knew even her name, and none knew more of her than her name. I doubt whether it would be possible to mention any other author of note, whose personal obscurity was so complete. I can think of none like her, but of many to contrast with her in that respect. Fanny Burney, afterwards Madame D'Arblay, was at an early age petted by Dr. Johnson, and introduced to the wits and scholars of the day at the tables of Mrs. Thrale and

Sir Joshua Reynolds. Anna Seward, in her self-constituted shrine at Lichfield, would have been miserable, had she not trusted that the eyes of all lovers of poetry were devoutly fixed on her. Joanna Baillie and Maria Edgeworth were indeed far from courting publicity; they loved the privacy of their own families, one with her brother and sister in their Hampstead villa, the other in her more distant retreat in Ireland; but fame pursued them, and they were the favourite correspondents of Sir Walter Scott. Crabbe, who was usually buried in a country parish, yet sometimes visited London, and dined at Holland House, and was received as a fellow-poet by Campbell, Moore, and Rogers; and on one memorable occasion he was Scott's guest at Edinburgh, and gazed with wondering eyes on the incongruous pageantry with which George IV. was entertained in that city. Even those great writers who hid themselves amongst lakes and mountains associated with each other; and though little seen by the world were so much in its thoughts that a new term, ' Lakers,' was coined to designate them. The chief part of Charlotte Brontë's life was spent in a wild solitude compared with which Steventon and Chawton might be considered to be in the gay world; and yet she attained to personal distinction which never fell to Jane's lot. When she visited her kind publisher in London, literary men and women were invited purposely to meet her : Thackeray bestowed upon her the honour of his notice ; and once in Willis's Rooms,* she had to walk shy and trembling through an avenue of lords and ladies, drawn up for the purpose of gazing at the author of ' Jane Eyre.' Miss Mitford, too, lived quietly in ' Our Village,' devoting her time and talents to the benefit of a father scarcely worthy of her ; but she did not live there unknown. Her tragedies gave her a name in London. She numbered Milman and Talfourd amongst her correspondents ; and her works were a passport to the society of many who would not otherwise have sought her. Hundreds admired Miss Mitford on account of her writings for one who ever connected the idea of Miss Austen with the press. A few years ago, a gentleman visiting Winchester Cathedral desired to be shown Miss Austen's grave. The verger, as he pointed it out, asked, ' Pray, sir, can you tell me whether there was anything particular about that lady ; so many people want to know where she was buried ? ' During her life the ignorance of the verger was shared by most people ; few knew that ' there was anything particular about that lady.'

It was not till towards the close of her life, when the last of the works that she saw published was in the press, that she received the only mark of distinction ever bestowed upon her ; and that was remarkable for the high quarter whence it emanated rather than for any actual increase of fame that it

* See Mrs. Gaskell's ' Life of Miss Brontë,' vol. ii. p. 215.

conferred. It happened thus. In the autumn of
1815 she nursed her brother Henry through a dan-
gerous fever and slow convalescence at his house in
Hans Place. He was attended by one of the Prince
Regent's physicians. All attempts to keep her
name secret had at this time ceased, and though it
had never appeared on a title-page, all who cared to
know might easily learn it : and the friendly physician was aware that his patient's nurse was the
author of ' Pride and Prejudice.' Accordingly he
informed her one day that the Prince was a great
admirer of her novels ; that he read them often, and
kept a set in every one of his residences ; that he
himself therefore had thought it right to inform his
Royal Highness that Miss Austen was staying in
London, and that the Prince had desired Mr.
Clarke, the librarian of Carlton House, to wait upon
her. The next day Mr. Clarke made his appearance,
and invited her to Carlton House, saying that he
had the Prince's instructions to show her the
library and other apartments, and to pay her every
possible attention. The invitation was of course
accepted, and during the visit to Carlton House
Mr. Clarke declared himself commissioned to say
that if Miss Austen had any other novel forthcoming
she was at liberty to dedicate it to the Prince.
Accordingly such a dedication was immediately
prefixed to ' Emma,' which was at that time in the
press.

Mr. Clarke was the brother of Dr. Clarke, the

traveller and mineralogist, whose life has been written by Bishop Otter. Jane found in him not only a very courteous gentleman, but also a warm admirer of her talents ; though it will be seen by his letters that he did not clearly apprehend the limits of her powers, or the proper field for their exercise. The following correspondence took place between them.

Feeling some apprehension lest she should make a mistake in acting on the verbal permission which she had received from the Prince, Jane addressed the following letter to Mr. Clarke :—

'Nov. 15, 1815.

'SIR,—I must take the liberty of asking you a question. Among the many flattering attentions which I received from you at Carlton House on Monday last was the information of my being at liberty to dedicate any future work to His Royal Highness the Prince Regent, without the necessity of any solicitation on my part. Such, at least, I believed to be your words ; but as I am very anxious to be quite certain of what was intended, I entreat you to have the goodness to inform me how such a permission is to be understood, and whether it is incumbent on me to show my sense of the honour, by inscribing the work now in the press to His Royal Highness ; I should be equally concerned to appear either presumptuous or un-grateful.'

The following gracious answer was returned by
Mr. Clarke, together with a suggestion which must
have been received with some surprise :—

'Carlton House, Nov. 16, 1815.

' DEAR MADAM,—It is certainly not *incumbent* on
you to dedicate your work now in the press to His
Royal Highness ; but if you wish to do the Regent
that honour either now or at any future period I am
happy to send you that permission, which need not
require any more trouble or solicitation on your part.

' Your late works, Madam, and in particular
" Mansfield Park," reflect the highest honour on
your genius and your principles. In every new
work your mind seems to increase its energy and
power of discrimination. The Regent has read and
admired all your publications.

' Accept my best thanks for the pleasure your
volumes have given me. In the perusal of them I
felt a great inclination to write and say so. And I
also, dear Madam, wished to be allowed to ask you
to delineate in some future work the habits of life,
and character, and enthusiasm of a clergyman, who
should pass his time between the metropolis and the
country, who should be something like Beattie's
Minstrel—

> Silent when glad, affectionate tho' shy,
>   And in his looks was most demurely sad ;
> And now he laughed aloud, yet none knew why.

Neither Goldsmith, nor La Fontaine in his
" Tableau de Famille," have in my mind quite

delineated an English clergyman, at least of the present day, fond of and entirely engaged in literature, no man's enemy but his own. Pray, dear Madam, think of these things.

> ' Believe me at all times with sincerity and respect, your faithful and obliged servant,
> ' J. S. CLARKE, Librarian.'

The following letter, written in reply, will show how unequal the author of ' Pride and Prejudice ' felt herself to delineating an enthusiastic clergyman of the present day, who should resemble Beattie's Minstrel :—

' Dec. 11.

' DEAR SIR,—My " Emma " is now so near publication that I feel it right to assure you of my not having forgotten your kind recommendation of an early copy for Carlton House, and that I have Mr. Murray's promise of its being sent to His Royal Highness, under cover to you, three days previous to the work being really out. I must make use of this opportunity to thank you, dear Sir, for the very high praise you bestow on my other novels. I am too vain to wish to convince you that you have praised them beyond their merits. My greatest anxiety at present is that this fourth work should not disgrace what was good in the others. But on this point I will do myself the justice to declare that, whatever may be my wishes for its success, I am strongly haunted with the idea that to those readers who have preferred " Pride and Prejudice " it will appear inferior in wit, and to those who have preferred " Mansfield Park " inferior in good sense. Such as it is, however, I hope you will do me the favour of accepting a copy. Mr. Murray will have directions for sending one. I am quite honoured by your thinking me capable of drawing such a clergy-man as you gave the sketch of in your note of Nov. 16th. But I assure you I am *not*. The comic part of the character I might be equal to, but not the good, the enthusiastic, the literary. Such a man's conversation must at times be on subjects of science and philosophy, of which I know nothing ; or at least be occasionally abundant in quotations and allusions which a woman who, like me, knows only her own mother tongue, and has read little in that, would be totally without the power of giving. A classical education, or at any rate a very extensive acquaintance with English literature, ancient and modern, appears to me quite indis-pensable for the person who would do any justice to your clergyman ; and I think I may boast myself to be, with all possible vanity, the most unlearned and uninformed female who ever dared to be an authoress.

> ' Believe me, dear Sir,
> ' Your obliged and faithful hum^{bl} Ser^t.
> ' JANE AUSTEN.'*

* It was her pleasure to boast of greater ignorance than she had any just claim to. She knew more than her mother tongue, for she knew a good deal of French and a little of Italian.

Mr. Clarke, however, was not to be discouraged from proposing another subject. He had recently been appointed chaplain and private English secretary to Prince Leopold, who was then about to be united to the Princess Charlotte ; and when he again wrote to express the gracious thanks of the Prince Regent for the copy of ' Emma ' which had been presented, he suggests that ' an historical romance illustrative of the august House of Cobourg would just now be very interesting,' and might very properly be dedicated to Prince Leopold. This was much as if Sir William Ross had been set to paint a great battle-piece ; and it is amusing to see with what grave civility she declined a proposal which must have struck her as ludicrous, in the following letter :—

' MY DEAR SIR,—I am honoured by the Prince's thanks and very much obliged to yourself for the kind manner in which you mention the work. I have also to acknowledge a former letter forwarded to me from Hans Place. I assure you I felt very grateful for the friendly tenor of it, and hope my silence will have been considered, as it was truly meant, to proceed only from an unwillingness to tax your time with idle thanks. Under every interesting circumstance which your own talents and literary labours have placed you in, or the favour of the Regent bestowed, you have my best wishes. Your recent appointments I hope are a step to something still better. In my opinion, the service of a court can hardly be too well paid, for immense must be the sacrifice of time and feeling required by it.

' You are very kind in your hints as to the sort of composition which might recommend me at present, and I am fully sensible that an historical romance, founded on the House of Saxe Cobourg, might be much more to the purpose of profit or popularity than such pictures of domestic life in country villages as I deal in. But I could no more write a romance than an epic poem. I could not sit seriously down to write a serious romance under any other motive than to save my life; and if it were indispensable for me to keep it up and never relax into laughing at myself or at other people, I am sure I should be hung before I had finished the first chapter. No, I must keep to my own style and go on in my own way; and though I may never succeed again in that, I am convinced that I should totally fail in any other.

' I remain, my dear Sir,

' Your very much obliged, and sincere friend,

' J. AUSTEN.

' Chawton, near Alton, April 1, 1816.'

Mr. Clarke should have recollected the warning of the wise man, ' Force not the course of the river.' If you divert it from the channel in which nature taught it to flow, and force it into one arbitrarily cut by yourself, you will lose its grace and beauty.

> But when his free course is not hindered,
> He makes sweet music with the enamelled stones,
> Giving a gentle kiss to every sedge
> He overtaketh in his pilgrimage :
> And so by many winding nooks he strays
> With willing sport.

All writers of fiction, who have genius strong enough to work out a course of their own, resist every attempt to interfere with its direction. No two writers could be more unlike each other than Jane Austen and Charlotte Brontë ; so much so that the latter was unable to understand why the former was admired, and confessed that she herself ' should hardly like to live with her ladies and gentlemen, in their elegant but confined houses ; ' but each writer equally resisted interference with her own natural style of composition. Miss Brontë, in reply to a friendly critic, who had warned her against being too melodramatic, and had ventured to propose Miss Austen's works to her as a study, writes thus :—

' Whenever I *do* write another book, I think I will have nothing of what you call " melodrama." I *think* so, but I am not sure. I *think*, too, I will endeavour to follow the counsel which shines out of Miss Austen's " mild eyes," to finish more, and be more subdued ; but neither am I sure of that. When authors write best, or, at least, when they write most fluently, an influence seems to waken in them which becomes their master—which will have its way—putting out of view all behests but its own, dictating certain words, and insisting on their being used, whether vehement or measured in their nature, new moulding characters, giving unthought of turns to incidents, rejecting carefully elaborated old ideas, and suddenly creating and adopting new ones. Is it not so? And should we try to counteract this influence? Can we indeed counteract it?'*

The playful raillery with which the one parries an attack on her liberty, and the vehement eloquence of the other in pleading the same cause and maintaining the independence of genius, are very characteristic of the minds of the respective writers.

The suggestions which Jane received as to the sort of story that she ought to write were, however, an amusement to her, though they were not likely to prove useful; and she has left amongst her papers one entitled, 'Plan of a novel according to hints from various quarters.' The names of some of those advisers are written on the margin of the manuscript opposite to their respective suggestions.

'Heroine to be the daughter of a clergyman, who after having lived much in the world had retired from it, and settled on a curacy with a very small fortune of his own. The most excellent man that can be imagined, perfect in character, temper, and manner, without the smallest drawback or peculiarity to prevent his being the most delightful companion to his daughter from one year's end to

* Mrs. Gaskell's 'Life of Miss Brontë,' vol. ii. p. 53.

the other. Heroine faultless in character, beautiful in person, and possessing every possible accomplishment. Book to open with father and daughter conversing in long speeches, elegant language, and a tone of high serious sentiment. The father induced, at his daughter's earnest request, to relate to her the past events of his life. Narrative to reach through the greater part of the first volume; as besides all the circumstances of his attachment to her mother, and their marriage, it will comprehend his going to sea as chaplain to a distinguished naval character about the court; and his going afterwards to court himself, which involved him in many interesting situations, concluding with his opinion of the benefits of tithes being done away with. . . . From this outset the story will proceed, and contain a striking variety of adventures. Father an exemplary parish priest, and devoted to literature; but heroine and father never above a fortnight in one place: he being driven from his curacy by the vile arts of some totally unprincipled and heartless young man, desperately in love with the heroine, and pursuing her with unrelenting passion. No sooner settled in one country of Europe, than they are compelled to quit it, and retire to another, always making new acquaintance, and always obliged to leave them. This will of course exhibit a wide variety of character. The scene will be for ever shifting from one set of people to another, but there will be no mixture, all the good will be unexceptionable in every respect. There will be no foibles or weaknesses but with the wicked, who will be completely depraved and infamous, hardly a resemblance of humanity left in them. Early in her career, the heroine must meet with the hero : all perfection, of course, and only prevented from paying his addresses to her by some excess of refinement. Wherever she goes, somebody falls in love with her, and she receives repeated offers of marriage, which she refers wholly to her father, exceedingly angry that *he* should not be the first applied to. Often carried away by the anti-hero, but rescued either by her father or the hero. Often reduced to support herself and her father by her talents, and work for her bread ; continually cheated, and defrauded of her hire ; worn down to a skeleton, and now and then starved to death. At last, hunted out of civilised society, denied the poor shelter of the humblest cottage, they are compelled to retreat into Kamtschatka, where the poor father quite worn down, finding his end approaching, throws himself on the ground, and after four or five hours of tender advice and parental admonition to his miserable child, expires in a fine burst of literary enthusiasm, intermingled with invectives against the holders of tithes. Heroine inconsolable for some time, but afterwards crawls back towards her former country, having at least twenty narrow escapes of falling into the hands of anti-hero ; and at last, in the very nick of time, turning a corner to avoid him, runs into the arms of the hero himself, who, having just shaken off the scruples which fettered him before, was at the very moment setting off in pursuit of her. The tenderest and completest *éclaircissement* takes place, and they are happily united. Throughout the whole work heroine to be in the most elegant society, and living in high style.'

Since the first publication of this memoir, Mr. Murray of Albemarle Street has very kindly sent to me copies of the following letters, which his father received from Jane Austen, when engaged in the publication of 'Emma.' The increasing cordiality of the letters shows that the author felt that her interests were duly cared for, and was glad to find herself in the hands of a publisher whom she could consider as a friend.

Her brother had addressed to Mr. Murray a strong complaint of the tardiness of a printer :—

' 23 Hans Place, Thursday, November 23 (1815).

' SIR,—My brother's note last Monday has been so fruitless, that I am afraid there can be but little chance of my writing to any good effect ; but yet I am so very much disappointed and vexed by the delays of the printers, that I cannot help begging to know whether there is no hope of their being quickened. Instead of the work being ready by the end of the present month, it will hardly, at the rate we now proceed, be finished by the end of the next; and as I expect to leave London early in December, it is

of consequence that no more time should be lost. Is
it likely that the printers will be influenced to
greater dispatch and punctuality by knowing that
the work is to be dedicated, by permission, to the
Prince Regent ? If you can make that circumstance
operate, I shall be very glad. My brother returns
' Waterloo ' with many thanks for the loan of it.
We have heard much of Scott's account of Paris.*
If it be not incompatible with other arrangements,
would you favour us with it, supposing you have
any set already opened ? You may depend upon its
being in careful hands.

'I remain, Sir, your obt· humble Set·

' J. AUSTEN.'

' Hans Place, December 11 (1815).

' DEAR SIR,—As I find that " Emma " is adver-
tised for publication as early as Saturday next, I
think it best to lose no time in settling all that
remains to be settled on the subject, and adopt this
method as involving the smallest tax on your time.

' In the first place, I beg you to understand that I
leave the terms on which the trade should be supplied with the work entirely to your judgment, en-
treating you to be guided in every such arrangement by your own experience of what is most likely
to clear off the edition rapidly. I shall be satisfied
with whatever you feel to be best. The title-page
must be " Emma, dedicated by permission to

* This must have been ' Paul's Letters to his Kinsfolk.'

H.R.H. the Prince Regent." And it is my particular wish that one set should be completed and
sent to H.R.H. two or three days before the work
is generally public. It should be sent under cover
to the Rev. J. S. Clarke, Librarian, Carlton House.
I shall subjoin a list of those persons to whom I
must trouble you to forward also a set each, when
the work is out ; all unbound, with " From the
Authoress " in the first page.

' I return you, with very many thanks, the books
you have so obligingly supplied me with. I am very
sensible, I assure you, of the attention you have
paid to my convenience and amusement. I return
also " Mansfield Park," as ready for a second
edition, I believe, as I can make it. I am in Hans
Place till the 16th. From that day inclusive, my
direction will be Chawton, Alton, Hants.

   ' I remain, dear Sir,

     ' Yr faithful humb. Servt.

       ' J. AUSTEN.

' I wish you would have the goodness to send a
line by the bearer, stating *the day* on which the set
will be ready for the Prince Regent.'

     ' Hans Place, December 11 (1815).

' DEAR SIR,—I am much obliged by yours, and
very happy to feel everything arranged to our
mutual satisfaction. As to my direction about the
title-page, it was arising from my ignorance only,
and from my having never noticed the proper place

for a dedication. I thank you for putting me right. Any deviation from what is usually done in such cases is the last thing I should wish for. I feel happy in having a friend to save me from the ill effect of my own blunder.

' Yours, dear Sir, &c.
' J. AUSTEN.'

' Chawton, April 1, 1816.

' DEAR SIR,—I return you the " Quarterly Review" with many thanks. The Authoress of " Emma " has no reason, I think, to complain of her treatment in it, except in the total omission of " Mansfield Park." I cannot but be sorry that so clever a man as the Reviewer of " Emma " should consider it as unworthy of being noticed. You will be pleased to hear that I have received the Prince's thanks for the *handsome* copy I sent him of " Emma." Whatever he may think of *my* share of the work, yours seems to have been quite right.

' In consequence of the late event in Henrietta Street, I must request that if you should at any time have anything to communicate by letter, you will be so good as to write by the post, directing to me (Miss J. Austen), Chawton, near Alton ; and that for anything of a larger bulk, you will add to the same direction, by *Collier's Southampton coach.*

' I remain, dear Sir,
' Yours very faithfully,
' J. AUSTEN.'

About the same time the following letters passed between the Countess of Morley and the writer of ' Emma.' I do not know whether they were personally acquainted with each other, nor in what this interchange of civilities originated :—

The Countess of Morley to Miss J. Austen.

' Saltram, December 27 (1815).

' MADAM,—I have been most anxiously waiting for an introduction to " Emma," and am infinitely obliged to you for your kind recollection of me, which will procure me the pleasure of her acquaintance some days sooner than I should otherwise have had it. I am already become intimate with the Woodhouse family, and feel that they will not amuse and interest me less than the Bennetts, Bertrams, Norrises, and all their admirable predecessors. I can give them no higher praise.

' I am, Madam, your much obliged

' F. MORLEY.'

Miss J. Austen to the Countess of Morley.

' MADAM,—Accept my thanks for the honour of your note, and for your kind disposition in favour of " Emma." In my present state of doubt as to her reception in the world, it is particularly gratifying to me to receive so early an assurance of your Ladyship's approbation. It encourages me to depend on

the same share of general good opinion which
" Emma's " predecessors have experienced, and
to believe that I have not yet, as almost every
writer of fancy does sooner or later, overwritten
myself.

' I am, Madam,

' Your obliged and faithful Servt.

' J. AUSTEN.

' December 31, 1815.'

CHAPTER VIII.

*Slow growth of her fame—Ill success of first attempts at publication—
Two Reviews of her works contrasted.*

SELDOM has any literary reputation been of such
slow growth as that of Jane Austen. Readers of
the present day know the rank that is generally
assigned to her. They have been told by Arch-
bishop Whately, in his review of her works, and by
Lord Macaulay, in his review of Madame D'Arblay's,
the reason why the highest place is to be awarded to
Jane Austen, as a truthful drawer of character, and
why she is to be classed with those who have
approached nearest, in that respect, to the great
master Shakspeare. They see her safely placed,
by such authorities, in her niche, not indeed
amongst the highest orders of genius, but in one
confessedly her own, in our British temple of
literary fame ; and it may be difficult to make them
believe how coldly her works were at first received,
and how few readers had any appreciation of their
peculiar merits. Sometimes a friend or neighbour,
who chanced to know of our connection with the
author, would condescend to speak with moderate
approbation of ' Sense and Sensibility,' or ' Pride
and Prejudice ' ; but if they had known that we, in

our secret thoughts, classed her with Madame
D'Arblay or Miss Edgeworth, or even with some
other novel writers of the day whose names are now
scarcely remembered, they would have considered it
an amusing instance of family conceit.   To the
multitude her works appeared tame and common-
place,* poor in colouring, and sadly deficient in
incident and interest.   It is true that we were
sometimes cheered by hearing that a different
verdict had been pronounced by more competent
judges : we were told how some great statesman or
distinguished poet held these works in high estimation ; we had the satisfaction of believing that they
were most admired by the best judges, and com-
forted ourselves with Horace's ' satis est Equitem
mihi plaudere.'   So much was this the case, that
one of the ablest men of my acquaintance † said, in
that kind of jest which has much earnest in it,
that he had established it in his own mind, as a new
test of ability, whether people *could* or *could not*
appreciate Miss Austen's merits.

* A greater genius than my aunt shared with her the imputation
of being *commonplace*. Lockhart, speaking of the low estimation in
which Scott's conversational powers were held in the literary and
scientific society of Edinburgh, says : ' I think the epithet most in
vogue concerning it was " commonplace." ' He adds, however, that
one of the most eminent of that society was of a different opinion,
' who, when some glib youth chanced to echo in his hearing the con-
solatory tenet of local mediocrity, answered quietly, " I have the
misfortune to think differently from you—in my humble opinion
Walter Scott's *sense* is a still more wonderful thing than his genius." '
—Lockhart's *Life of Scott*, vol. iv. chap. v.

† The late Mr. R. H. Cheney.

But though such golden opinions were now and then gathered in, yet the wide field of public taste yielded no adequate return either in praise or profit. Her reward was not to be the quick return of the cornfield, but the slow growth of the tree which is to endure to another generation. Her first attempts at publication were very discouraging. In November, 1797, her father wrote the following letter to Mr. Cadell :—

'Sir,—I have in my possession a manuscript novel, comprising 3 vols., about the length of Miss Burney's "Evelina." As I am well aware of what consequence it is that a work of this sort sh^d make its first appearance under a respectable name, I apply to you. I shall be much obliged therefore if you will inform me whether you choose to be concerned in it, what will be the expense of publishing it at the author's risk, and what you will venture to advance for the property of it, if on perusal it is approved of. Should you give any encouragement, I will send you the work.

'I am, Sir, your humble Servant,
'GEORGE AUSTEN.'

'Steventon, near Overton, Hants,
'1st Nov. 1797.'

This proposal was declined by return of post ! The work thus summarily rejected must have been ' Pride and Prejudice.'

The fate of ' Northanger Abbey ' was still more

humiliating. It was sold, in 1803, to a publisher in
Bath, for ten pounds, but it found so little favour in
his eyes, that he chose to abide by his first loss
rather than risk farther expense by publishing such
a work. It seems to have lain for many years unnoticed in his drawers ; somewhat as the first
chapters of ' Waverley ' lurked forgotten amongst
the old fishing-tackle in Scott's cabinet. Tilneys,
Thorpes, and Morlands consigned apparently to
eternal oblivion ! But when four novels of steadily
increasing success had given the writer some confidence in herself, she wished to recover the copyright of this early work. One of her brothers undertook the negotiation. He found the purchaser very
willing to receive back his money, and to resign all
claim to the copyright. When the bargain was
concluded and the money paid, but not till then,
the negotiator had the satisfaction of informing him
that the work which had been so lightly esteemed
was by the author of ' Pride and Prejudice.' I do
not think that she was herself much mortified by
the want of early success. She wrote for her own
amusement. Money, though acceptable, was not
necessary for the moderate expenses of her quiet
home. Above all, she was blessed with a cheerful
contented disposition, and an humble mind ;
and so lowly did she esteem her own claims, that
when she received 150*l.* from the sale of ' Sense and
Sensibility,' she considered it a prodigious recom-
pense for that which had cost her nothing. It can-

not be supposed, however, that she was altogether insensible to the superiority of her own workman-ship over that of some contemporaries who were then enjoying a brief popularity. Indeed a few touches in the following extracts from two of her letters show that she was as quicksighted to absur-dities in composition as to those in living persons.

' Mr. C.'s opinion is gone down in my list ; but as my paper relates only to " Mansfield Park," I may fortunately excuse myself from entering Mr. D's. I will redeem my credit with him by writing a close imitation of " Self-Control," as soon as I can. I will improve upon it. My heroine shall not only be wafted down an American river in a boat by herself. She shall cross the Atlantic in the same way ; and never stop till she reaches Gravesend.'

' We have got " Rosanne " in our Society, and find it much as you describe it ; very good and clever, but tedious. Mrs. Hawkins' great excellence is on serious subjects. There are some very delight-ful conversations and reflections on religion : but on lighter topics I think she falls into many absurdities ; and, as to love, her heroine has very comical feelings. There are a thousand improba-bilities in the story. Do you remember the two Miss Ormsdens introduced just at last? Very flat and unnatural. Mad^{elle.} Cossart is rather my passion.'

Two notices of her works appeared in the ' Quarterly Review. ' One in October 1815, and another, more than three years after her death, in

January 1821. The latter article is known to have
been from the pen of Whately, afterwards Arch-
bishop of Dublin.* They differ much from each
other in the degree of praise which they award, and
I think also it may be said, in the ability with which
they are written. The first bestows some approval,
but the other expresses the warmest admiration.
One can scarcely be satisfied with the critical
acumen of the former writer, who, in treating of
' Sense and Sensibility,' takes no notice whatever
of the vigour with which many of the characters are
drawn, but declares that ' the interest and *merit*
of the piece depends *altogether* upon the behaviour
of the elder sister ! ' Nor is he fair when, in ' Pride
and Prejudice,' he represents Elizabeth's change of
sentiments towards Darcy as caused by the sight of
his house and grounds. But the chief discrepancy
between the two reviewers is to be found in their
appreciation of the commonplace and silly characters to be found in these novels. On this point the
difference almost amounts to a contradiction, such
as one sometimes sees drawn up in parallel columns,
when it is desired to convict some writer or some

* Lockhart had supposed that this article had been written by
Scott, because it exactly accorded with the opinions which Scott had
often been heard to express, but he learned afterwards that it had been
written by Whately ; and Lockhart, who became the Editor of the
Quarterly, must have had the means of knowing the truth. (See Lockhart's *Life of Sir Walter Scott*, vol. v. p. 158.) I remember that, at the
time when the review came out, it was reported in Oxford that Whately
had written the article at the request of the lady whom he afterwards
married.

statesman of inconsistency. The Reviewer, in 1815, says : ' The faults of these works arise from the minute detail which the author's plan comprehends. Characters of folly or simplicity, such as those of old Woodhouse and Miss Bates, are ridiculous when first presented, but if too often brought forward, or too long dwelt on, their prosing is apt to become as tiresome in fiction as in real society.' The Reviewer, in 1821, on the contrary, singles out the fools as especial instances of the writer's abilities, and declares that in this respect she shows a regard to character hardly exceeded by Shakspeare himself. These are his words : ' Like him (Shakspeare) she shows as admirable a discrimination in the character of fools as of people of sense ; a merit which is far from common. To invent indeed a conversation full of wisdom or of wit requires that the writer should himself possess ability ; but the converse does not hold good, it is no fool that can describe fools well ; and many who have succeeded pretty well in painting superior characters have failed in giving individuality to those weaker ones which it is necessary to introduce in order to give a faithful representation of real life : they exhibit to us mere folly in the abstract, forgetting that to the eye of the skilful naturalist the insects on a leaf present as wide differences as exist between the lion and the elephant. Slender, and Shallow, and Aguecheek, as Shakspeare has painted them, though equally fools, resemble one another

no more than Richard, and Macbeth, and Julius
Cæsar ; and Miss Austen's* Mrs. Bennet, Mr. Rush-
worth, and Miss Bates are no more alike than her
Darcy, Knightley, and Edmund Bertram. Some
have complained indeed of finding her fools too
much like nature, and consequently tiresome.
There is no disputing about tastes ; all we can say is,
that such critics must (whatever deference they
may outwardly pay to received opinions) find
the " Merry Wives of Windsor " and " Twelfth
Night " very tiresome ; and that those who look
with pleasure at Wilkie's pictures, or those of the
Dutch school, must admit that excellence of imitation may confer attraction on that which would be
insipid or disagreeable in the reality. Her minute-
ness of detail has also been found fault with ; but
even where it produces, at the time, a degree of
tediousness, we know not whether that can justly
be reckoned a blemish, which is absolutely essential
to a very high excellence. Now it is absolutely
impossible, without this, to produce that thorough
acquaintance with the characters which is necessary
to make the reader heartily interested in them.
Let any one cut out from the " Iliad " or from
Shakspeare's plays everything (we are far from
saying that either might not lose some parts with
advantage, but let him reject everything) which is
absolutely devoid of importance and interest *in*

---

* In transcribing this passage I have taken the liberty so far to correct it as to spell her name properly with an ' e.'

itself; and he will find that what is left will have lost more than half its charms. We are convinced that some writers have diminished the effect of their works by being scrupulous to admit nothing into them which had not some absolute and independent merit. They have acted like those who strip off the leaves of a fruit tree, as being of themselves good for nothing, with the view of securing more nourishment to the fruit, which in fact cannot attain its full maturity and flavour without them.'

The world, I think, has endorsed the opinion of the later writer ; but it would not be fair to set down the discrepancy between the two entirely to the discredit of the former. The fact is that, in the course of the intervening five years, these works had been read and reread by many leaders in the literary world. The public taste was forming itself all this time, and ' grew by what it fed on.' These novels belong to a class which gain rather than lose by frequent perusals, and it is probable that each Reviewer represented fairly enough the prevailing opinions of readers in the year when each wrote.

Since that time, the testimonies in favour of Jane Austen's works have been continual and almost unanimous. They are frequently referred to as models; nor have they lost their first distinction of being especially acceptable to minds of the highest order. I shall indulge myself by collecting into the next chapter instances of the homage paid to her by such persons.

CHAPTER IX.

Opinions expressed by eminent persons—Opinions of others of less eminence—Opinion of American readers.

INTO this list of the admirers of my Aunt's works, I admit those only whose eminence will be universally acknowledged. No doubt the number might have been increased.

Southey, in a letter to Sir Egerton Brydges, says : ' You mention Miss Austen. Her novels are more true to nature, and have, for my sympathies, passages of finer feeling than any others of this age. She was a person of whom I have heard so well and think so highly, that I regret not having had an opportunity of testifying to her the respect which I felt for her.'

It may be observed that Southey had probably heard from his own family connections of the charm of her private character. A friend of hers, the daughter of Mr. Bigge Wither, of Manydown Park near Basingstoke, was married to Southey's uncle, the Rev. Herbert Hill, who had been useful to his nephew in many ways, and especially in supplying him with the means of attaining his extensive knowledge of Spanish and Portuguese literature. Mr. Hill had been Chaplain to the British Factory at Lisbon, where Southey visited him and had the use of a library in those languages which his uncle had collected. Southey himself continually mentions his uncle Hill in terms of respect and gratitude.

S. T. Coleridge would sometimes burst out into high encomiums of Miss Austen's novels as being, ' in their way, perfectly genuine and individual productions.'

I remember Miss Mitford's saying to me : ' I would almost cut off one of my hands, if it would enable me to write like your aunt with the other.'

The biographer of Sir J. Mackintosh says : ' Something recalled to his mind the traits of character which are so delicately touched in Miss Austen's novels. . . He said that there was genius in sketching out that new kind of novel. . . He was vexed for the credit of the " Edinburgh Review " that it had left her unnoticed.* . . The " Quarterly " had done her more justice. . . It was impossible for a foreigner to understand fully the merit of her works. Madame de Staël, to whom he had recommended one of her novels, found no interest in it ; and in her note to him in reply said it was " vulgaire " : and yet, he said, nothing could be more true than what he wrote in answer : " There is no book which that word would so little suit." . . . Every village could furnish matter for a novel to Miss Austen. She did not need the common

* Incidentally she had received high praise in Lord Macaulay's Review of Madame D'Arblay's Works in the ' Edinburgh.'

materials for a novel, strong emotions, or strong incidents.' *

It was not, however, quite impossible for a foreigner to appreciate these works ; for Mons. Guizot writes thus : ' I am a great novel reader, but I seldom read German or French novels. The characters are too artificial. My delight is to read English novels, particularly those written by women. " C'est toute une école de morale." Miss Austen, Miss Ferrier, &c., form a school which in the excellence and profusion of its productions resembles the cloud of dramatic poets of the great Athenian age.'

In the ' Keepsake ' of 1825 the following lines appeared, written by Lord Morpeth, afterwards seventh Earl of Carlisle, and Lord-Lieutenant of Ireland, accompanying an illustration of a lady reading a novel.

> Beats thy quick pulse o'er Inchbald's thrilling leaf,
> Brunton's high moral, Opie's deep wrought grief ?
> Has the mild chaperon claimed thy yielding heart,
> Carroll's dark page, Trevelyan's gentle art ?
> Or is it thou, all perfect Austen ? Here
> Let one poor wreath adorn thy early bier,
> That scarce allowed thy modest youth to claim
> Its living portion of thy certain fame !
> Oh ! Mrs. Bennet ! Mrs. Norris too !
> While memory survives we'll dream of you.
> And Mr. Woodhouse, whose abstemious lip
> Must thin, but not too thin, his gruel sip.

---

* *Life of Sir J. Mackintosh*, vol. ii. p. 472.

Miss Bates, our idol, though the village bore ;
And Mrs. Elton, ardent to explore.
While the clear style flows on without pretence,
With unstained purity, and unmatched sense :
Or, if a sister e'er approached the throne,
She called the rich ' inheritance ' her own.

The admiration felt by Lord Macaulay would probably have taken a very practical form, if his life had been prolonged. I have the authority of his sister, Lady Trevelyan, for stating that he had intended to undertake the task upon which I have ventured. He purposed to write a memoir of Miss Austen, with criticisms on her works, to prefix it to a new edition of her novels, and from the proceeds of the sale to erect a monument to her memory in Winchester Cathedral. Oh ! that such an idea had been realised ! That portion of the plan in which Lord Macaulay's success would have been most certain might have been almost sufficient for his object. A memoir written by him would have been a monument.

I am kindly permitted by Sir Henry Holland to give the following quotation from his printed but unpublished recollections of his past life :—

' I have the picture still before me of Lord Holland lying on his bed, when attacked with gout, his admirable sister, Miss Fox, beside him reading aloud, as she always did on these occasions, some one of Miss Austen's novels, of which he was never wearied. I well recollect the time when these charming novels, almost unique in their style of humour, burst suddenly on the world. It was sad that their writer did not live to witness the growth of her fame.'

My brother-in-law, Sir Denis Le Marchant, has supplied me with the following anecdotes from his own recollections :—

'When I was a student at Trinity College, Cambridge, Mr. Whewell, then a Fellow and afterwards Master of the College, often spoke to me with admiration of Miss Austen's novels. On one occasion I said that I had found " Persuasion " rather dull. He quite fired up in defence of it, insisting that it was the most beautiful of her works. This accomplished philosopher was deeply versed in works of fiction. I recollect his writing to me from Caernarvon, where he had the charge of some pupils, that he was weary of *his* stay, for he had read the circulating library twice through.

'During a visit I paid to Lord Lansdowne, at Bowood, in 1846, one of Miss Austen's novels became the subject of conversation and of praise, especially from Lord Lansdowne, who observed that one of the circumstances of his life which he looked back upon with vexation was that Miss Austen should once have been living some weeks in his neighbourhood without his knowing it.

'I have heard Sydney Smith, more than once, dwell with eloquence on the merits of Miss Austen's novels. He told me he should have enjoyed giving

her the pleasure of reading her praises in the
" Edinburgh Review." " Fanny Price " was one
of his prime favourites.'

I close this list of testimonies, this long ' Catena
Patrum,' with the remarkable words of Sir Walter
Scott, taken from his diary for March 14, 1826 : *
' Read again, for the third time at least, Miss
Austen's finely written novel of " Pride and Prejudice." That young lady had a talent for describing
the involvements and feelings and characters of
ordinary life, which is to me the most wonderful I
ever met with. The big Bow-Wow strain I can do
myself like any now going ; but the exquisite touch
which renders ordinary common-place things and
characters interesting from the truth of the description and the sentiment is denied to me. What a
pity such a gifted creature died so early ! ' The
well-worn condition of Scott's own copy of these
works attests that they were much read in his
family. When I visited Abbotsford, a few years
after Scott's death, I was permitted, as an unusual
favour, to take one of these volumes in my hands.
One cannot suppress the wish that she had lived to
know what such men thought of her powers, and
how gladly they would have cultivated a personal
acquaintance with her. I do not think that it
would at all have impaired the modest simplicity
of her character ; or that we should have lost

* Lockhart's *Life of Scott*, vol. vi. chap. vii.

our own dear ' Aunt Jane ' in the blaze of literary
fame.

It may be amusing to contrast with these testimonies from the great, the opinions expressed by
other readers of more ordinary intellect.   The
author herself has left a list of criticisms which it
had been her amusement to collect, through means
of her friends.   This list contains much of warm-
hearted sympathising praise, interspersed with
some opinions which may be considered surprising.

One lady could say nothing better of ' Mansfield
Park,' than that it was ' a mere novel.'

Another owned that she thought ' Sense and
Sensibility ' and ' Pride and Prejudice ' downright
nonsense ; but expected to like ' Mansfield Park '
better, and having finished the first volume, hoped
that she had got through the worst.

Another did not like ' Mansfield Park.'   Nothing
interesting in the characters.   Language poor.

One gentleman read the first and last chapters of
' Emma,' but did not look at the rest, because he
had been told that it was not interesting.

The opinions of another gentleman about ' Emma '
were so bad that they could not be reported to the
author.

' Quot homines, tot sententiæ.'

Thirty-five years after her death there came also a
voice of praise from across the Atlantic.   In 1852
the following letter was received by her brother Sir
Francis Austen :—

'Boston, Massachusetts, U.S.A.
6th Jan. 1852.

' Since high critical authority has pronounced the delineations of character in the works of Jane Austen second only to those of Shakspeare, trans-atlantic admiration appears superfluous ; yet it may not be uninteresting to her family to receive an assurance that the influence of her genius is exten-sively recognised in the American Republic, even by the highest judicial authorities. The late Mr. Chief Justice Marshall, of the supreme Court of the United States, and his associate Mr. Justice Story, highly estimated and admired Miss Austen, and to them we owe our introduction to her society. For many years her talents have brightened our daily path, and her name and those of her characters are familiar to us as " household words." We have long wished to express to some of her family the senti-ments of gratitude and affection she has inspired, and request more information relative to her life than is given in the brief memoir prefixed to her works.

' Having accidentally heard that a brother of Jane Austen held a high rank in the British Navy, we have obtained his address from our friend Admiral Wormley, now resident in Boston, and we trust this expression of our feeling will be received by her relations with the kindness and urbanity characteristic of Admirals of *her creation*. Sir Francis Austen, or one of his family, would confer a great favour by complying with our request. The autograph of his sister, or a few lines in her hand-writing, would be placed among our chief treasures.

' The family who delight in the companionship of Jane Austen, and who present this petition, are of English origin. Their ancestor held a high rank among the first emigrants to New England, and his name and character have been ably represented by his descendants in various public stations of trust and responsibility to the present time in the colony and state of Massachusetts. A letter addressed to Miss Quincey, care of the Honble Josiah Quincey, Boston, Massachusetts, would reach its destination.'

Sir Francis Austen returned a suitable reply to this application ; and sent a long letter of his sister's, which, no doubt, still occupies the place of honour promised by the Quincey family.

CHAPTER X.

Observations on the Novels.

It is not the object of these memoirs to attempt a criticism on Jane Austen's novels. Those particulars only have been noticed which could be illustrated by the circumstances of her own life ; but I now desire to offer a few observations on them, and especially on one point, on which my age renders me a competent witness—the fidelity with which they represent the opinions and manners of the class of society in which the author lived early in this century. They do this the more faithfully on account of the very deficiency with which they have been sometimes charged—namely, that they make no attempt to raise the standard of human life, but merely represent it as it was. They certainly were not written to support any theory or inculcate any particular moral, except indeed the great moral which is to be equally gathered from an observation of the course of actual life—namely, the superiority of high over low principles, and of greatness over littleness of mind. These writings are like photographs, in which no feature is softened ; no ideal expression is introduced, all is the unadorned reflection of the natural object ; and the value of such a faithful likeness must increase as time gradually works more and more changes in the face of society itself. A remarkable instance of this is to be found in her portraiture of the clergy. She was the daughter and the sister of clergymen, who certainly were not low specimens of their order : and she has chosen three of her heroes from that profession ; but no one in these days can think that either Edmund Bertram or Henry Tilney had adequate ideas of the duties of a parish minister. Such, however, were the opinions and practice then prevalent among respectable and conscientious clergymen before their minds had been stirred, first by the Evangelical, and afterwards by the High Church movement which this century has witnessed. The country may be congratulated which, on looking back to such a fixed landmark, can find that it has been advancing instead of receding from it.

The long interval that elapsed between the completion of ' Northanger Abbey ' in 1798, and the commencement of ' Mansfield Park ' in 1811, may sufficiently account for any difference of style which may be perceived between her three earlier and her three later productions. If the former showed quite as much originality and genius, they may perhaps be thought to have less of the faultless finish and high polish which distinguish the latter. The characters of the John Dashwoods, Mr. Collins, and the Thorpes stand out from the canvas with a vigour and originality which cannot be surpassed ;

but I think that in her last three works are to be
found a greater refinement of taste, a more nice
sense of propriety, and a deeper insight into the
delicate anatomy of the human heart, marking the
difference between the brilliant girl and the mature
woman. Far from being one of those who have
over-written themselves, it may be affirmed that her
fame would have stood on a narrower and less firm
basis, if she had not lived to resume her pen at
Chawton.

Some persons have surmised that she took her
characters from individuals with whom she had
been acquainted. They were so life-like that it was
assumed that they must once have lived, and have
been transferred bodily, as it were, into her pages.
But surely such a supposition betrays an ignorance
of the high prerogative of genius to create out of its
own resources imaginary characters, who shall be
true to nature and consistent in themselves. Perhaps, however, the distinction between keeping
true to nature and servilely copying any one specimen of it is not always clearly apprehended. It is
indeed true, both of the writer and of the painter,
that he can use only such lineaments as exist, and
as he has observed to exist, in living objects ;
otherwise he would produce monsters instead of
human beings ; but in both it is the office of high
art to mould these features into new combinations,
and to place them in the attitudes, and impart to
them the expressions which may suit the purposes

of the artist ; so that they are nature, but not
exactly the same nature which had come before his
eyes ; just as honey can be obtained only from the
natural flowers which the bee has sucked ; yet it is
not a reproduction of the odour or flavour of any
particular flower, but becomes something different
when it has gone through the process of transforma-
tion which that little insect is able to effect. Hence,
in the case of painters, arises the superiority of
original compositions over portrait painting.
Reynolds was exercising a higher faculty when he
designed Comedy and Tragedy contending for
Garrick, than when he merely took a likeness of
that actor. The same difference exists in writings
between the original conceptions of Shakspeare and
some other creative geniuses, and such full-length
likenesses of individual persons, ' The Talking
Gentleman ' for instance, as are admirably drawn
by Miss Mitford. Jane Austen's powers, whatever
may be the degree in which she possessed them,
were certainly of that higher order. She did not
copy individuals, but she invested her own creations
with individuality of character. A reviewer in the
' Quarterly ' speaks of an acquaintance who, ever
since the publication of ' Pride and Prejudice,' had
been called by his friends Mr. Bennet, but the
author did not know him. Her own relations never
recognised any individual in her characters ; and
I can call to mind several of her acquaintance whose
peculiarities were very tempting and easy to be

caricatured of whom there are no traces in her pages. She herself, when questioned on the subject by a friend, expressed a dread of what she called such an 'invasion of social proprieties.' She said that she thought it quite fair to note peculiarities and weaknesses, but that it was her desire to create, not to reproduce ; 'besides,' she added, ' I am too proud of my gentlemen to admit that they were only Mr. A. or Colonel B.' She did not, however, suppose that her imaginary characters were of a higher order than are to be found in nature ; for she said, when speaking of two of her great favourites, Edmund Bertram and Mr. Knightley : ' They are very far from being what I know English gentlemen often are.'

She certainly took a kind of parental interest in the beings whom she had created, and did not dismiss them from her thoughts when she had finished her last chapter. We have seen, in one of her letters, her personal affection for Darcy and Elizabeth ; and when sending a copy of ' Emma ' to a friend whose daughter had been lately born, she wrote thus : ' I trust you will be as glad to see my " Emma," as I shall be to see your Jemima.' She was very fond of Emma, but did not reckon on her being a general favourite ; for, when commencing that work, she said, ' I am going to take a heroine whom no one but myself will much like.' She would, if asked, tell us many little particulars about the subsequent career of some of her people. In this traditionary way we

learned that Miss Steele never succeeded in catching
the Doctor ; that Kitty Bennet was satisfactorily
married to a clergyman near Pemberley, while
Mary obtained nothing higher than one of her uncle
Philip's clerks, and was content to be considered a
star in the society of Meriton ; that the ' considerable sum ' given by Mrs. Norris to William Price
was one pound ; that Mr. Woodhouse survived his
daughter's marriage, and kept her and Mr.
Knightley from settling at Donwell, about two
years ; and that the letters placed by Frank
Churchill before Jane Fairfax, which she swept
away unread, contained the word ' pardon.' Of the
good people in ' Northanger Abbey ' and ' Persuasion ' we know nothing more than what is
written : for before those works were published
their author had been taken away from us, and all
such amusing communications had ceased for ever.

CHAPTER XI.

Declining health of Jane Austen—Elasticity of her spirits—Her resignation and humility—Her death.

EARLY in the year 1816 some family troubles disturbed the usually tranquil course of Jane Austen's life ; and it is probable that the inward malady, which was to prove ultimately fatal, was already felt by her ; for some distant friends,* whom she visited in the spring of that year, thought that her health was somewhat impaired, and observed that she went about her old haunts, and recalled old recollections connected with them in a particular manner, as if she did not expect ever to see them again. It is not surprising that, under these circumstances, some of her letters were of a graver tone than had been customary with her, and expressed resignation rather than cheerfulness. In reference to these troubles in a letter to her brother Charles, after mentioning that she had been laid up with an attack of bilious fever, she says : ' I live up stairs for the present and am coddled. I am the only one of the party who has been so silly, but a weak body must excuse weak nerves.' And again, to another correspondent : ' But I am getting too near com-

* The Fowles, of Kintbury, in Berkshire.

plaint ; it has been the appointment of God, however secondary causes may have operated.' But
the elasticity of her spirits soon recovered their
tone. It was in the latter half of that year that she
addressed the two following lively letters to a
nephew, one while he was at Winchester School, the
other soon after he had left it :—

'Chawton, July 9, 1816.

' My Dear E.—Many thanks. A thank for every
line, and as many to Mr. W. Digweed for coming.
We have been wanting very much to hear of your
mother, and are happy to find she continues to
mend, but her illness must have been a very serious
one indeed. When she is really recovered, she ought
to try change of air, and come over to us. Tell your
father that I am very much obliged to him for his
share of your letter, and most sincerely join in the
hope of her being eventually much the better for
her present discipline. She has the comfort moreover of being confined in such weather as gives one
little temptation to be out. It is really too bad, and
has been too bad for a long time, much worse than
any one *can* bear, and I begin to think it will never
be fine again. This is a *finesse* of mine, for I have
often observed that if one writes about the weather,
it is generally completely changed before the letter
is read. I wish it may prove so now, and that when
Mr. W. Digweed reaches Steventon to-morrow, he
may find you have had a long series of hot dry

weather. We are a small party at present, only
grandmamma, Mary Jane, and myself. Yalden's
coach cleared off the rest yesterday. I am glad you
recollected to mention your being come home.* My
heart began to sink within me when I had got so far
through your letter without its being mentioned. I
was dreadfully afraid that you might be detained at
Winchester by severe illness, confined to your bed
perhaps, and quite unable to hold a pen, and only
dating from Steventon in order, with a mistaken
sort of tenderness, to deceive me. But now I have
no doubt of your being at home. I am sure you
would not say it so seriously unless it actually were
so. We saw a countless number of post-chaises full
of boys pass by yesterday morning †—full of future
heroes, legislators, fools, and villains. You have
never thanked me for my last letter, which went by
the cheese. I cannot bear not to be thanked. You
will not pay us a visit yet of course ; we must not
think of it. Your mother must get well first, and
you must go to Oxford and *not* be elected ; after
that a little change of scene may be good for you,
and your physicians I hope will order you to the sea,
or to a house by the side of a very considerable
pond.‡ Oh ! it rains again. It beats against the

---

* It seems that her young correspondent, after dating from his
home, had been so superfluous as to state in his letter that he was
returned home, and thus to have drawn on himself this banter.

† The road by which many Winchester boys returned home ran
close to Chawton Cottage.

‡ There was, though it exists no longer, a pond close to Chawton
Cottage, at the junction of the Winchester and Gosport roads.

window. Mary Jane and I have been wet through once already to-day ; we set off in the donkey-carriage for Farringdon, as I wanted to see the improvement Mr. Woolls is making, but we were obliged to turn back before we got there, but not soon enough to avoid a pelter all the way home. We met Mr. Woolls. I talked of its being bad weather for the hay, and he returned me the comfort of its being much worse for the wheat. We hear that Mrs. S. does not quit Tangier : why and wherefore ? Do you know that our Browning is gone ? You must prepare for a William when you come, a good-looking lad, civil and quiet, and seeming likely to do. Good bye. I am sure Mr. W. D.* will be astonished at my writing so much, for the paper is so thin that he will be able to count the lines if not to read them.

' Yours affec^{ly},

' Jane Austen.'

In the next letter will be found her description of her own style of composition, which has already appeared in the notice prefixed to 'Northanger Abbey' and 'Persuasion' :—

' Chawton, Monday, Dec. 16th (1816).

' My Dear E.,—One reason for my writing to you now is, that I may have the pleasure of directing to you Esqre. I give you joy of having left Winchester.

---

* Mr. Digweed, who conveyed the letters to and from Chawton, was the gentleman named in page [22], as renting the old manor-house and the large farm at Steventon.

Now you may own how miserable you were there ; now it will gradually all come out, your crimes and your miseries—how often you went up by the Mail to London and threw away fifty guineas at a tavern, and how often you were on the point of hanging yourself, restrained only, as some ill-natured aspersion upon poor old Winton has it, by the want of a tree within some miles of the city. Charles Knight and his companions passed through Chawton about 9 this morning ; later than it used to be. Uncle Henry and I had a glimpse of his handsome face, looking all health and good humour. I wonder when you will come and see us. I know what I rather speculate upon, but shall say nothing. We think uncle Henry in excellent looks. Look at him this moment, and think so too, if you have not done it before ; and we have the great comfort of seeing decided improvement in uncle Charles, both as to health, spirits, and appearance. And they are each of them so agreeable in their different way, and harmonise so well, that their visit is thorough en-joyment. Uncle Henry writes very superior sermons. You and I must try to get hold of one or two, and put them into our novels : it would be a fine help to a volume ; and we could make our heroine read it aloud on a Sunday evening, just as well as Isabella Wardour, in the " Antiquary," is made to read the " History of the Hartz Demon " in the ruins of St. Ruth, though I believe, on re-collection, Lovell is the reader. By the bye, my dear E., I am quite concerned for the loss your mother mentions in her letter. Two chapters and a half to be missing is monstrous ! It is well that *I* have not been at Steventon lately, and therefore cannot be suspected of purloining them : two strong twigs and a half towards a nest of my own would have been something. I do not think, however, that any theft of that sort would be really very useful to me. What should I do with your strong, manly, vigorous sketches, full of variety and glow ? How could I possibly join them on to the little bit (two inches wide) of ivory on which I work with so fine a brush, as produces little effect after much labour ?

' You will hear from uncle Henry how well Anna is. She seems perfectly recovered. Ben was here on Saturday, to ask uncle Charles and me to dine with them, as to-morrow, but I was forced to decline it, the walk is beyond my strength (though I am otherwise very well), and this is not a season for donkey-carriages ; and as we do not like to spare uncle Charles, he has declined it too. *Tuesday.* Ah, ah ! Mr. E. I doubt your seeing uncle Henry at Steventon to-day. The weather will prevent your expecting him, I think. Tell your father, with aunt Cass's love and mine, that the pickled cucumbers are extremely good, and tell him also— " tell him what you will." No, don't tell him what you will, but tell him that grandmamma begs him to make Joseph Hall pay his rent, if he can.

' You must not be tired of reading the word *uncle*, for I have not done with it. Uncle Charles thanks your mother for her letter ; it was a great pleasure to him to know that the parcel was received and gave so much satisfaction, and he begs her to be so good as to give three shillings for him to Dame Staples, which shall be allowed for in the payment of her debt here.

' Adieu, Amiable ! I hope Caroline behaves well to you.

' Yours affec^{ly},

' J. AUSTEN.'

I cannot tell how soon she was aware of the serious nature of her malady. By God's mercy it was not attended with much suffering ; so that she was able to tell her friends as in the foregoing letter, and perhaps sometimes to persuade herself that, excepting want of strength, she was ' otherwise very well ; ' but the progress of the disease became more and more manifest as the year advanced. The usual walk was at first shortened, and then discontinued ; and air was sought in a donkey-carriage. Gradually, too, her habits of activity within the house ceased, and she was obliged to lie down much. The sitting-room contained only one sofa, which was frequently occupied by her mother, who was more than seventy years old. Jane would never use it, even in her mother's absence ; but she contrived a sort of couch for herself with two or three chairs, and was pleased to say that this arrangement was more comfortable to her than a real sofa. Her reasons for this might have been left to be guessed, but for the importunities of a little niece, which obliged her to explain that if she herself had shown any inclination to use the sofa, her mother might have scrupled being on it so much as was good for her.

It is certain, however, that the mind did not share in this decay of the bodily strength. ' Persuasion ' was not finished before the middle of August in that year ; and the manner in which it was then completed affords proof that neither the critical nor the creative powers of the author were at all impaired. The book had been brought to an end in July ; and the re-engagement of the hero and heroine effected in a totally different manner in a scene laid at Admiral Croft's lodgings. But her performance did not satisfy her. She thought it tame and flat, and was desirous of producing something better. This weighed upon her mind, the more so probably on account of the weak state of her health ; so that one night she retired to rest in very low spirits. But such depression was little in accordance with her nature, and was soon shaken off. The next morning she awoke to more cheerful views and brighter inspirations : the sense of power revived ; and imagination resumed its course. She cancelled the condemned chapter, and wrote two others, entirely different, in its stead. The result is that we

possess the visit of the Musgrove party to Bath ;
the crowded and animated scenes at the White
Hart Hotel ; and the charming conversation between Capt. Harville and Anne Elliot, overheard by
Capt. Wentworth, by which the two faithful
lovers were at last led to understand each other's
feelings. The tenth and eleventh chapters of
' Persuasion ' then, rather than the actual winding-
up of the story, contain the latest of her printed
compositions, her last contribution to the entertainment of the public. Perhaps it may be thought
that she has seldom written anything more brilliant;
and that, independent of the original manner in
which the *dénouement* is brought about, the pictures
of Charles Musgrove's goodnatured boyishness and
of his wife's jealous selfishness would have been
incomplete without these finishing strokes. The
cancelled chapter exists in manuscript. It is
certainly inferior to the two which were substituted
for it : but it was such as some writers and some
readers might have been contented with ; and it
contained touches which scarcely any other hand
could have given, the suppression of which may
be almost a matter of regret.*

The following letter was addressed to her friend
Miss Bigg, then staying at Streatham with her
sister, the wife of the Reverend Herbert Hill, uncle
of Robert Southey. It appears to have been written

* This cancelled chapter is now printed, in compliance with the
requests addressed to me from several quarters.

three days before she began her last work, which
will be noticed in another chapter ; and shows that
she was not at that time aware of the serious nature
of her malady :—

'My dear Alethea,—I think it time there
should be a little writing between us, though I believe the epistolary debt is on *your* side, and I hope
this will find all the Streatham party well, neither
carried away by the flood, nor rheumatic through
the damps. Such mild weather is, you know, delightful to *us*, and though we have a great many
ponds, and a fine running stream through the
meadows on the other side of the road, it is nothing
but what beautifies us and does to talk of. *I* have
certainly gained strength through the winter and
am not far from being well ; and I think I understand my own case now so much better than I did,
as to be able by care to keep off any serious return of
illness. I am convinced that *bile* is at the bottom of
all I have suffered, which makes it easy to know
how to treat myself. You will be glad to hear thus
much of me, I am sure. We have just had a few
days' visit from Edward, who brought us a good
account of his father, and the very circumstance of
his coming at all, of his father's being able to spare
him, is itself a good account. He grows still, and
still improves in appearance, at least in the estimation of his aunts, who love him better and better,

as they see the sweet temper and warm affections of
the boy confirmed in the young man : I tried hard
to persuade him that he must have some message
for William,* but in vain. . . . This is not a time of
year for donkey-carriages, and our donkeys are
necessarily having so long a run of luxurious idle-
ness that I suppose we shall find they have forgotten much of their education when we use
them again.   We do not use two at once however ;
don't imagine such excesses. . . Our own new clergyman † is expected here very soon, perhaps in time to
assist Mr. Papillon on Sunday.   I shall be very glad
when the first hearing is over.   It will be a nervous
hour for our pew, though we hear that he acquits
himself with as much ease and collectedness, as if
he had been used to it all his life.   We have no
chance we know of seeing you between Streatham
and Winchester : you go the other road and are
engaged to two or three houses ; if there should be
any change, however, you know how welcome you
would be. . . . We have been reading the " Poet's
Pilgrimage to Waterloo,' and generally with much
approbation.   Nothing will please all the world, you
know ; but parts of it suit me better than much
that he has written before.   The opening—*the
proem* I believe he calls it—is very beautiful.   Poor
man ! one cannot but grieve for the loss of the son

* Miss Bigg's nephew, the present Sir William Heathcote, of
Hursley.

† Her brother Henry, who had been ordained late in life.

so fondly described. Has he at all recovered it ?
What do Mr. and Mrs. Hill know about his present
state ?

' Yours aff^{ly},

' J. AUSTEN.

' The real object of this letter is to ask you for a
receipt, but I thought it genteel not to let it appear
early. We remember some excellent orange wine at
Manydown, made from Seville oranges, entirely or
chiefly. I should be very much obliged to you for
the receipt, if you can command it within a few
weeks.'

On the day before, January 23rd, she had written
to her niece in the same hopeful tone : ' I feel myself getting stronger than I was, and can so perfectly walk *to* Alton, *or* back again without fatigue,
that I hope to be able to do *both* when summer
comes.'

Alas ! summer came to her only on her death-
bed. March 17th is the last date to be found in the
manuscript on which she was engaged ; and as the
watch of the drowned man indicates the time of his
death, so does this final date seem to fix the period
when her mind could no longer pursue its accustomed course.

And here I cannot do better than quote the words
of the niece to whose private records of her aunt's
life and character I have been so often indebted :—

' I do not know how early the alarming symptoms of her malady came on. It was in the following March that I had the first idea of her being seriously ill. It had been settled that about the end of that month, or the beginning of April, I should spend a few days at Chawton, in the absence of my father and mother, who were just then engaged with Mrs. Leigh Perrot in arranging her late husband's affairs ; but Aunt Jane became too ill to have me in the house, and so I went instead to my sister Mrs. Lefroy at Wyards'. The next day we walked over to Chawton to make enquiries after our aunt. She was then keeping her room, but said she would see us, and we went up to her. She was in her dressing gown, and was sitting quite like an invalid in an arm-chair, but she got up and kindly greeted us, and then, pointing to seats which had been arranged for us by the fire, she said, " There is a chair for the married lady, and a little stool for you, Caroline." * It is strange, but those trifling words were the last of hers that I can re-member, for I retain no recollection of what was said by anyone in the conversation that ensued. I was struck by the alteration in herself. She was very pale, her voice was weak and low, and there was about her a general appearance of debility and suffering ; but I have been told that she never had much acute pain. She was not equal to the exertion of talking to us, and our visit to the sick room was a very short one, Aunt Cassandra soon

* The writer was at that time under twelve years old.

taking us away. I do not suppose we stayed
a quarter of an hour; and I never saw Aunt Jane
again.'

In May 1817 she was persuaded to remove to
Winchester, for the sake of medical advice from
Mr. Lyford. The Lyfords have, for some generations, maintained a high character in Winchester
for medical skill, and the Mr. Lyford of that day
was a man of more than provincial reputation, in
whom great London practitioners expressed confidence. Mr. Lyford spoke encouragingly. It was
not, of course, his business to extinguish hope in his
patient, but I believe that he had, from the first,
very little expectation of a permanent cure. All
that was gained by the removal from home was the
satisfaction of having done the best that could be
done, together with such alleviations of suffering as
superior medical skill could afford.

Jane and her sister Cassandra took lodgings in
College Street. They had two kind friends living
in the Close, Mrs. Heathcote and Miss Bigg, the
mother and aunt of the present Sir Wm. Heathcote
of Hursley, between whose family and ours a close
friendship has existed for several generations.
These friends did all that they could to promote the
comfort of the sisters, during that sad sojourn in
Winchester, both by their society, and by supplying
those little conveniences in which a lodging-house
was likely to be deficient. It was shortly after
settling in these lodgings that she wrote to a nephew

the following characteristic letter, no longer, alas !
in her former strong, clear hand.

' Mrs. David's, College St., Winton,
Tuesday, May 27th.

' There is no better way, my dearest E., of thank-
ing you for your affectionate concern for me during
my illness than by telling you myself, as soon as
possible, that I continue to get better.   I will not
boast of my handwriting ; neither that nor my face
have yet recovered their proper beauty, but in other
respects I gain strength very fast.   I am now out of
bed from 9 in the morning to 10 at night : upon
the sofa, it is true, but I eat my meals with aunt
Cassandra in a rational way, and can employ myself,
and walk from one room to another.   Mr. Lyford
says he will cure me, and if he fails, I shall draw up
a memorial and lay it before the Dean and Chapter,
and have no doubt of redress from that pious,
learned, and disinterested body.   Our lodgings are
very comfortable.   We have a neat little drawing-
room with a bow window overlooking Dr. Gabell's
garden.*   Thanks to the kindness of your father and
mother in sending me their carriage, my journey
hither on Saturday was performed with very little
fatigue, and had it been a fine day, I think I should
have felt none ; but it distressed me to see uncle
Henry and Wm. Knight, who kindly attended us on

---

* It was the corner house in College Street, at the entrance to
Commoners.

horseback, riding in the rain almost the whole way. We expect a visit from them to-morrow, and hope they will stay the night ; and on Thursday, which is a confirmation and a holiday, we are to get Charles out to breakfast. We have had but one visit from *him*, poor fellow, as he is in sick-room, but he hopes to be out to-night. We see Mrs. Heathcote every day, and William is to call upon us soon. God bless you, my dear E. If ever you are ill, may you be as tenderly nursed as I have been. May the same blessed alleviations of anxious, sympathising friends be yours : and may you possess, as I dare say you will, the greatest blessing of all in the consciousness of not being unworthy of their love. *I* could not feel this.

' Your very affec^{te} Aunt,

' J. A.'

The following extract from a letter which has been before printed, written soon after the former, breathes the same spirit of humility and thankfulness :—

' I will only say further that my dearest sister, my tender, watchful, indefatigable nurse, has not been made ill by her exertions. As to what I owe her, and the anxious affection of all my beloved family on this occasion, I can only cry over it, and pray God to bless them more and more.'

Throughout her illness she was nursed by her sister, often assisted by her sister-in-law, my mother.

Both were with her when she died. Two of her brothers, who were clergymen, lived near enough to Winchester to be in frequent attendance, and to administer the services suitable for a Christian's death-bed. While she used the language of hope to her correspondents, she was fully aware of her danger, though not appalled by it. It is true that there was much to attach her to life. She was happy in her family ; she was just beginning to feel confidence in her own success ; and, no doubt, the exercise of her great talents was an enjoyment in itself. We may well believe that she would gladly have lived longer ; but she was enabled without dismay or complaint to prepare for death. She was a humble, believing Christian. Her life had been passed in the performance of home duties, and the cultivation of domestic affections, without any self-seeking or craving after applause. She had always sought, as it were by instinct, to promote the happiness of all who came within her influence, and doubtless she had her reward in the peace of mind which was granted her in her last days. Her sweetness of temper never failed. She was ever considerate and grateful to those who attended on her. At times, when she felt rather better, her playfulness of spirit revived, and she amused them even in their sadness. Once, when she thought herself near her end, she said what she imagined might be her last words to those around her, and particularly thanked her sister-in-law for being with

her, saying : ' You have always been a kind sister
to me, Mary.' When the end at last came, she sank
rapidly, and on being asked by her attendants
whether there was anything that she wanted, her
reply was, ' *Nothing but death.*' These were her last
words.   In quietness and peace she breathed her
last on the morning of July 18, 1817.

On the 24th of that month she was buried in
Winchester Cathedral, near the centre of the north
aisle, almost opposite to the beautiful chantry tomb
of William of Wykeham.   A large slab of black
marble in the pavement marks the place.   Her own
family only attended the funeral.   Her sister returned to her desolated home, there to devote
herself, for ten years, to the care of her aged mother;
and to live much on the memory of her lost sister, till
called many years later to rejoin her.   Her brothers
went back sorrowing to their several homes.   They
were very fond and very proud of her.   They were
attached to her by her talents, her virtues, and her
engaging manners ;   and each loved afterwards to
fancy a resemblance in some niece or daughter of
his own to the dear sister Jane, whose perfect equal
they yet never expected to see.

CHAPTER XII.

The Cancelled Chapter (Chap. X.) of ' Persuasion.'

WITH all this knowledge of Mr. Elliot and this
authority to impart it, Anne left Westgate
Buildings, her mind deeply busy in revolving what
she had heard, feeling, thinking, recalling, and
foreseeing everything, shocked at Mr. Elliot,
sighing over future Kellynch, and pained for Lady
Russell, whose confidence in him had been entire.
The embarrassment which must be felt from this
hour in his presence ! How to behave to him ?
How to get rid of him ? What to do by any of the
party at home ? Where to be blind ? Where to be
active ? It was altogether a confusion of images and
doubts—a perplexity, an agitation which she could
not see the end of. And she was in Gay Street, and
still so much engrossed that she started on being
addressed by Admiral Croft, as if he were a person
unlikely to be met there. It was within a few steps
of his own door.

' You are going to call upon my wife,' said he.
' She will be very glad to see you.'

Anne denied it.

' No ! she really had not time, she was in her way
home ; ' but while she spoke the Admiral had
stepped back and knocked at the door, calling out,

' Yes, yes ; do go in ; she is all alone ; go in and rest yourself.'

Anne felt so little disposed at this time to be in company of any sort, that it vexed her to be thus constrained, but she was obliged to stop.

' Since you are so very kind,' said she, ' I will just ask Mrs. Croft how she does, but I really cannot stay five minutes. You are sure she is quite alone ? '

The possibility of Captain Wentworth had occurred ; and most fearfully anxious was she to be assured—either that he was within, or that he was not—*which* might have been a question.

' Oh yes ! quite alone, nobody but her mantua-maker with her, and they have been shut up together this half-hour, so it must be over soon.'

' Her mantuamaker ! Then I am sure my calling now would be most inconvenient. Indeed you must allow me to leave my card and be so good as to explain it afterwards to Mrs. Croft.'

' No, no, not at all—not at all—she will be very happy to see you. Mind, I will not swear that she has not something particular to say to you, but *that* will all come out in the right place. I give no hints. Why, Miss Elliot, we begin to hear strange things of you (smiling in her face). But you have not much the look of it, as grave as a little judge ! '

Anne blushed.

' Aye, aye, that will do now, it is all right. I thought we were not mistaken.'

She was left to guess at the direction of his suspicions ; the first wild idea had been of some disclosure from his brother-in-law, but she was ashamed the next moment, and felt how far more probable it was that he should be meaning Mr. Elliot. The door was opened, and the man evidently beginning to *deny* his mistress, when the sight of his master stopped him. The Admiral enjoyed the joke exceedingly. Anne thought his triumph over Stephen rather too long. At last, however, he was able to invite her up stairs, and stepping before her said, ' I will just go up with you myself and show you in. I cannot stay, because I must go to the Post-Office, but if you will only sit down for five minutes I am sure Sophy will come, and you will find nobody to disturb you— there is nobody but Frederick here,' opening the door as he spoke. Such a person to be passed over as nobody to *her* ! After being allowed to feel quite secure, indifferent, at her ease, to have it burst on her that she was to be the next moment in the same room with him ! No time for recollection ! for planning behaviour or regulating manners ! There was time only to turn pale before she had passed through the door, and met the astonished eyes of Captain Wentworth, who was sitting by the fire, pretending to read, and prepared for no greater surprise than the Admiral's hasty return.

Equally unexpected was the meeting on each side. There was nothing to be done, however, but to stifle feelings, and to be quietly polite, and the Admiral was too much on the alert to leave any troublesome pause. He repeated again what he had said before about his wife and everybody, insisted on Anne's sitting down and being perfectly comfortable—was sorry he must leave her himself, but was sure Mrs. Croft would be down very soon, and would go upstairs and give her notice directly. Anne *was* sitting down, but now she arose, again to entreat him not to interrupt Mrs. Croft and re-urge the wish of going away and calling another time. But the Admiral would not hear of it ; and if she did not return to the charge with unconquerable perseverance, or did not with a more passive determination walk quietly out of the room (as certainly she might have done), may she not be pardoned ? If she *had* no horror of a few minutes' tête-à-tête with Captain Wentworth, may she not be pardoned for not wishing to give him the idea that she had ? She reseated herself, and the Admiral took leave, but on reaching the door, said—

' Frederick, a word with *you* if you please.'

Captain Wentworth went to him, and instantly, before they were well out of the room, the Admiral continued—

' As I am going to leave you together, it is but fair I should give you something to talk of ; and so, if you please—— '

Here the door was very firmly closed, she could guess by which of the two—and she lost entirely

what immediately followed, but it was impossible
for her not to distinguish parts of the rest, for the
Admiral, on the strength of the door's being shut,
was speaking without any management of voice,
though she could hear his companion trying to
check him. She could not doubt their being
speaking of her. She heard her own name and
Kellynch repeatedly. She was very much disturbed. She knew not what to do, or what to
expect, and among other agonies felt the possibility
of Captain Wentworth's not returning into the
room at all, which, after her consenting to stay,
would have been—too bad for language. They
seemed to be talking of the Admiral's lease of
Kellynch. She heard him say something of the
lease being signed—or not signed—*that* was not
likely to be a very agitating subject, but then
followed—

'I hate to be at an uncertainty. I must know at
once. Sophy thinks the same.'

Then in a lower tone Captain Wentworth seemed
remonstrating, wanting to be excused, wanting to
put something off.

'Phoo, phoo,' answered the Admiral, 'now is the
time; if you will not speak, I will stop and speak
myself.'

'Very well, sir, very well, sir,' followed with some
impatience from his companion, opening the door
as he spoke—

'You will then, you promise you will?' replied

the Admiral in all the power of his natural voice, unbroken even by one thin door.

' Yes, sir, yes.' And the Admiral was hastily left, the door was closed, and the moment arrived in which Anne was alone with Captain Wentworth.

She could not attempt to see how he looked, but he walked immediately to a window as if irresolute and embarrassed, and for about the space of five seconds she repented what she had done—censured it as unwise, blushed over it as indelicate. She longed to be able to speak of the weather or the concert, but could only compass the relief of taking a newspaper in her hand. The distressing pause was over, however ; he turned round in half a minute, and coming towards the table where she sat, said in a voice of effort and constraint—

' You must have heard too much already, Madam, to be in any doubt of my having promised Admiral Croft to speak to you on a particular subject, and this conviction determines me to do so, however repugnant to my—to all my sense of propriety to be taking so great a liberty ! You will acquit me of impertinence I trust, by considering me as speaking only for another, and speaking by necessity ; and the Admiral is a man who can never be thought impertinent by one who knows him as you do. His intentions are always the kindest and the best, and you will perceive he is actuated by none other in the application which I am now, with—with very peculiar feelings—obliged to make.' He stopped, but merely to recover breath, not seeming to expect any answer. Anne listened as if her life depended on the issue of his speech. He proceeded with a forced alacrity :—

'The Admiral, Madam, was this morning confidently informed that you were—upon my soul, I am quite at a loss, ashamed (breathing and speaking quickly)—the awkwardness of *giving* information of this kind to one of the parties—you can be at no loss to understand me. It was very confidently said that Mr. Elliot—that everything was settled in the family for a union between Mr. Elliot and yourself. It was added that you were to live at Kellynch —that Kellynch was to be given up. This the Admiral knew could not be correct. But it occurred to him that it might be the *wish* of the parties. And my commission from him, Madam, is to say, that if the family wish is such, his lease of Kellynch shall be cancelled, and he and my sister will provide themselves with another home, without imagining themselves to be doing anything which under similar circumstances would not be done for *them*. This is all, Madam. A very few words in reply from you will be sufficient. That *I* should be the person commissioned on this subject is extraordinary ! and believe me, Madam, it is no less painful. A very few words, however, will put an end to the awkwardness and distress we may *both* be feeling.'

Anne spoke a word or two, but they were unintelligible ; and before she could command herself, he

added, ' If you will only tell me that the Admiral
may address a line to Sir Walter, it will be enough.
Pronounce only the words, *he may*, and I shall immediately follow him with your message.'

' No, Sir,' said Anne ; ' there is no message. You
are misin—the Admiral is misinformed. I do justice
to the kindness of his intentions, but he is quite mistaken. There is no truth in any such report.'

He was a moment silent. She turned her eyes
towards him for the first time since his re-entering
the room. His colour was varying, and he was
looking at her with all the power and keenness
which she believed no other eyes than his possessed.

' No truth in any such report ? ' he repeated.
' No truth in any *part* of it ? '

' None.'

He had been standing by a chair, enjoying the
relief of leaning on it, or of playing with it. He now
sat down, drew it a little nearer to her, and looked
with an expression which had something more than
penetration in it—something softer. Her countenance did not discourage. It was a silent but a
very powerful dialogue ; on his supplication, on hers
acceptance. Still a little nearer, and a hand taken
and pressed ; and ' Anne, my own dear Anne ! '
bursting forth in all the fulness of exquisite feeling,
—and all suspense and indecision were over. They
were re-united. They were restored to all that had
been lost. They were carried back to the past with
only an increase of attachment and confidence, and

only such a flutter of present delight as made them little fit for the interruption of Mrs. Croft when she joined them not long afterwards. *She*, probably, in the observations of the next ten minutes saw something to suspect ; and though it was hardly possible for a woman of her description to wish the mantuamaker had imprisoned her longer, she might be very likely wishing for some excuse to run about the house, some storm to break the windows above, or a summons to the Admiral's shoemaker below. Fortune favoured them all, however, in another way, in a gentle, steady rain, just happily set in as the Admiral returned and Anne rose to go. She was earnestly invited to stay dinner. A note was despatched to Camden Place, and she staid—staid till ten at night ; and during that time the husband and wife, either by the wife's contrivance, or by simply going on in their usual way, were frequently out of the room together—gone upstairs to hear a noise, or downstairs to settle their accounts, or upon the landing to trim the lamp. And these precious moments were turned to so good an account that all the most anxious feelings of the past were gone through. Before they parted at night, Anne had the felicity of being assured that in the first place (so far from being altered for the worse), she had gained inexpressibly in personal loveliness ; and that as to character, hers was now fixed on his mind as *perfection* itself, maintaining the just medium of fortitude and gentleness—that he had never ceased to love and prefer her, though it had been only at Uppercross that he had learnt to do her justice, and only at Lyme that he had begun to understand his own feelings ; that at Lyme he had received lessons of more than one kind—the passing admiration of Mr. Elliot had at least *roused* him, and the scene on the Cobb, and at Captain Harville's, had fixed her superiority. In his preceding attempts to attach himself to Louisa Musgrove (the attempts of anger and pique), he protested that he had continually felt the impossibility of really caring for Louisa, though till *that day*, till the leisure for reflection which followed it, he had not understood the perfect excellence of the mind with which Louisa's could so ill bear comparison ; or the perfect, the unrivalled hold it possessed over his own. There he had learnt to distinguish between the steadiness of principle and the obstinacy of self-will, between the darings of heedlessness and the resolution of a collected mind ; there he had seen everything to exalt in his estimation the woman he had lost, and there had begun to deplore the pride, the folly, the madness of resentment, which had kept him from trying to regain her when thrown in his way. From that period to the present had his penance been the most severe. He had no sooner been free from the horror and remorse attending the first few days of Louisa's accident, no sooner had begun to feel himself alive again, than he had begun to feel himself, though alive, not at liberty.

He found that he was considered by his friend Harville an engaged man. The Harvilles entertained not a doubt of a mutual attachment between him and Louisa ; and though this to a degree was contradicted instantly, it yet made him feel that perhaps by *her* family, by everybody, by *herself* even, the same idea might be held, and that he was not *free* in honour, though if such were to be the conclusion, too free alas ! in heart. He had never thought justly on this subject before, and he had not sufficiently considered that his excessive intimacy at Uppercross must have its danger of ill consequence in many ways ; and that while trying whether he could attach himself to either of the girls, he might be exciting unpleasant reports if not raising unrequited regard.

He found too late that he had entangled himself, and that precisely as he became thoroughly satisfied of his not *caring* for Louisa at all, he must regard himself as bound to her if her feelings for him were what the Harvilles supposed. It determined him to leave Lyme, and await her perfect recovery elsewhere. He would gladly weaken by any *fair* means whatever sentiment or speculations concerning them might exist ; and he went therefore into Shropshire, meaning after a while to return to the Crofts at Kellynch, and act as he found requisite.

He had remained in Shropshire, lamenting the blindness of his own pride and the blunders of his own calculations, till at once released from Louisa by the astonishing felicity of her engagement with Benwick.

Bath—Bath had instantly followed in *thought*, and not long after in *fact*. To Bath—to arrive with hope, to be torn by jealousy at the first sight of Mr. Elliot ; to experience all the changes of each at the concert ; to be miserable by the morning's circumstantial report, to be now more happy than language could express, or any heart but his own be capable of.

He was very eager and very delightful in the description of what he had felt at the concert ; the evening seemed to have been made up of exquisite moments. The moment of her stepping forward in the octagon room to speak to him, the moment of Mr. Elliot's appearing and tearing her away, and one or two subsequent moments, marked by returning hope or increasing despondency, were dwelt on with energy.

' To see you,' cried he, ' in the midst of those who could not be my well-wishers ; to see your cousin close by you, conversing and smiling, and feel all the horrible eligibilities and proprieties of the match ! To consider it as the certain wish of every being who could hope to influence you ! Even if your own feelings were reluctant or indifferent, to consider what powerful support would be his ! Was it not enough to make the fool of me which I appeared ? How could I look on without agony ? Was not the very sight of the friend who sat behind you ; was not the recollection of what had been, the knowledge of her influence, the indelible, immovable impression of what persuasion had once done—was it not all against me ? '

' You should have distinguished,' replied Anne. ' You should not have suspected me now ; the case so different, and my age so different. If I was wrong in yielding to persuasion once, remember it was to persuasion exerted on the side of safety, not of risk. When I yielded, I thought it was to duty ; but no duty could be called in aid here. In marrying a man indifferent to me, all risk would have been incurred, and all duty violated.'

' Perhaps I ought to have reasoned thus,' he replied ; ' but I could not. I could not derive benefit from the late knowledge I had acquired of your character. I could not bring it into play ; it was overwhelmed, buried, lost in those earlier feelings which I had been smarting under year after year. I could think of you only as one who had yielded, who had given me up, who had been influenced by anyone rather than by me. I saw you with the very person who had guided you in that year of misery. I had no reason to believe her of less authority now. The force of habit was to be added.'

' I should have thought,' said Anne, ' that my manner to yourself might have spared you much or all of this.'

' No, no ! Your manner might be only the ease

which your engagement to another man would give. I left you in this belief; and yet—I was determined to see you again. My spirits rallied with the morning, and I felt that I had still a motive for remaining here. The Admiral's news, indeed, was a revulsion; since that moment I have been divided what to do, and had it been confirmed, this would have been my last day in Bath.'

There was time for all this to pass, with such interruptions only as enhanced the charm of the communication, and Bath could hardly contain any other two beings at once so rationally and so rapturously happy as during that evening occupied the sofa of Mrs. Croft's drawing-room in Gay Street.

Captain Wentworth had taken care to meet the Admiral as he returned into the house, to satisfy him as to Mr. Elliot and Kellynch; and the delicacy of the Admiral's good-nature kept him from saying another word on the subject to Anne. He was quite concerned lest he might have been giving her pain by touching on a tender part—who could say? She might be liking her cousin better than he liked her; and, upon recollection, if they had been to marry at all, why should they have waited so long? When the evening closed, it is probable that the Admiral received some new ideas from his wife, whose particularly friendly manner in parting with her gave Anne the gratifying persuasion of her seeing and approving. It had been such a day to Anne; the hours which had passed since her leaving Camden Place had done so much ! She was almost bewildered—almost too happy in looking back. It was necessary to sit up half the night, and lie awake the remainder, to comprehend with composure her present state, and pay for the overplus of bliss by headache and fatigue.

Then follows Chapter XI., *i. e.* XII. in the published book and at the end is written—

Finis, July 18, 1816.

CHAPTER XIII.

The Last Work.

JANE AUSTEN was taken from us : how much un-exhausted talent perished with her, how largely she might yet have contributed to the entertainment of her readers, if her life had been prolonged, cannot be known ; but it is certain that the mine at which she had so long laboured was not worked out, and that she was still diligently employed·in collecting fresh materials from it. ' Persuasion ' had been finished in August 1816 ; some time was probably given to correcting it for the press ; but on the 27th of the following January, according to the date on her own manuscript, she began a new novel, and worked at it up to the 17th of March. The chief part of this manuscript is written in her usual firm and neat hand, but some of the latter pages seem to have been first traced in pencil, probably when she was too weak to sit long at her desk, and written over in ink afterwards. The quantity produced does not indicate any decline of power or industry, for in those seven weeks twelve chapters had been completed. It is more difficult to judge of the quality of a work so little advanced. It had received no name ; there was scarcely any indication what the course of the story was to be, nor was any heroine yet perceptible, who, like Fanny Price, or Anne Elliot, might draw round her the sympathies of the reader. Such an unfinished fragment cannot be presented to the public ; but I am persuaded that some of Jane Austen's admirers will be glad to learn something about the latest creations which were forming themselves in her mind ; and therefore, as some of the principal characters were already sketched in with a vigorous hand, I will try to give an idea of them, illustrated by extracts from the work.

The scene is laid at Sanditon, a village on the Sussex coast, just struggling into notoriety as a bathing-place, under the patronage of the two principal proprietors of the parish, Mr. Parker and Lady Denham.

Mr. Parker was an amiable man, with more enthusiasm than judgment, whose somewhat shallow mind overflowed with the one idea of the prosperity of Sanditon, together with a jealous contempt of the rival village of Brinshore, where a similar attempt was going on. To the regret of his much-enduring wife, he had left his family mansion, with all its ancestral comforts of gardens, shrubberies, and shelter, situated in a valley some miles inland, and had built a new residence—a Trafalgar House—on the bare brow of the hill overlooking Sanditon and the sea, exposed to every wind that blows ; but he will confess to no discomforts, nor suffer his family to feel any from the change. The following extract brings him before the reader, mounted on his hobby :—

' He wanted to secure the promise of a visit, and to get as many of the family as his own house would hold to follow him to Sanditon as soon as possible ; and, healthy as all the Heywoods undeniably were, he foresaw that every one of them would be bene-fitted by the sea. He held it indeed as certain that no person, however upheld for the present by for-tuitous aids of exercise and spirit in a semblance of health, could be really in a state of secure and per-manent health without spending at least six weeks by the sea every year. The sea air and sea-bathing together were nearly infallible ; one or other of them being a match for every disorder of the stomach, the lungs, or the blood. They were anti-spasmodic, anti-pulmonary, anti-bilious, and anti-rheumatic. Nobody could catch cold by the sea ; nobody wanted appetite by the sea ; nobody wanted spirits ; nobody wanted strength. They were healing, softening, relaxing, fortifying, and bracing, seemingly just as was wanted ; sometimes one, sometimes the other. If the sea breeze failed, the sea-bath was the certain corrective ; and when bathing disagreed, the sea breeze was evidently designed by nature for the cure. His eloquence, however, could not prevail. Mr. and Mrs. Heywood never left home. . . . The maintenance, education, and fitting out of fourteen children demanded a very quiet, settled, careful course of life ; and obliged them to be stationary and healthy at Willingden. What prudence had at first enjoined was now rendered pleasant by habit. They never left home, and they had a gratification in saying so.'

Lady Denham's was a very different character. She was a rich vulgar widow, with a sharp but narrow mind, who cared for the prosperity of Sanditon only so far as it might increase the value of her own property. She is thus described :—

'Lady Denham had been a rich Miss Brereton, born to wealth, but not to education. Her first husband had been a Mr. Hollis, a man of considerable property in the country, of which a large share of the parish of Sanditon, with manor and mansion-house, formed a part. He had been an elderly man when she married him ; her own age about thirty. Her motives for such a match could be little understood at the distance of forty years, but she had so well nursed and pleased Mr. Hollis that at his death he left her everything—all his estates, and all at her disposal. After a widowhood of some years she had been induced to marry again. The late Sir Harry Denham, of Denham Park, in the neighbourhood of Sanditon, succeeded in removing her and her large income to his own domains ; but he could not succeed in the views of permanently enriching his family which were attributed to him. She had been too wary to put anything out of her own power, and when, on Sir Harry's death, she returned again to her own house at Sanditon, she was said to have made this boast, " that though she had *got* nothing but her title from the family, yet she had *given* nothing for it." For the title it was to be supposed that she married.

'Lady Denham was indeed a great lady, beyond the common wants of society; for she had many thousands a year to bequeath, and three distinct sets of people to be courted by :—her own relations, who might very reasonably wish for her original thirty thousand pounds among them; the legal heirs of Mr. Hollis, who might hope to be more indebted to *her* sense of justice than he had allowed them to be to *his*; and those members of the Denham family for whom her second husband had hoped to make a good bargain. By all these, or by branches of them, she had, no doubt, been long and still continued to be well attacked; and of these three divisions Mr. Parker did not hesitate to say that Mr. Hollis's kindred were the least in favour, and Sir Harry Denham's the most. The former, he believed, had done themselves irremediable harm by expressions of very unwise resentment at the time of Mr. Hollis's death : the latter, to the advantage of being the remnant of a connection which she certainly valued, joined those of having been known to her from their childhood, and of being always at hand to pursue their interests by seasonable attentions. But another claimant was now to be taken into account : a young female relation whom Lady Denham had been induced to receive into her family. After having always protested against any such addition, and often enjoyed the repeated defeat she had given to every attempt of her own relations to introduce ' this young lady, or that young lady,' as a companion at Sanditon House, she had brought back with her from London last Michaelmas a Miss Clara Brereton, who bid fair to vie in favour with Sir Edward Denham, and to secure for herself and her family that share of the accumulated property which they had certainly the best right to inherit.'

Lady Denham's character comes out in a conversation which takes place at Mr. Parker's teatable.

' The conversation turned entirely upon Sanditon, its present number of visitants, and the chances of a good season. It was evident that Lady Denham had more anxiety, more fears of loss than her coadjutor. She wanted to have the place fill faster, and seemed to have many harassing apprehensions of the lodgings being in some instances underlet. To a report that a large boarding-school was expected she replies, ' Ah, well, no harm in that. They will stay their six weeks, and out of such a number who knows but some may be consumptive, and want asses' milk ; and I have two milch asses at this very time. But perhaps the little Misses may hurt the furniture. I hope they will have a good sharp governess to look after them.' But she wholly disapproved of Mr. Parker's wish to secure the residence of a medical man amongst them. ' Why, what should we do with a doctor here ? It would only be encouraging our servants and the poor to fancy themselves ill, if there was a doctor at hand. Oh, pray let us have none of that tribe at Sanditon : we go on very well as we are. There is the sea, and the downs, and my milch asses : and I have told Mrs. Whitby that if anybody enquires for a chamber horse, they may be supplied at a fair rate (poor Mr. Hollis's chamber horse, as good as new) ; and what can people want more ? I have lived seventy good years in the world, and never took physic, except twice : and never saw the face of a doctor in all my life on my own account ; and I really believe if my poor dear Sir Harry had never seen one neither, he would have been alive now. Ten fees, one after another, did the men take who sent him out of the world. I beseech you, Mr. Parker, no doctors here.'

This lady's character comes out more strongly in a conversation with Mr. Parker's guest, Miss Charlotte Heywood. Sir Edward Denham with his sister Esther and Clara Brereton have just left them.

' Charlotte accepted an invitation from Lady Denham to remain with her on the terrace, when the others adjourned to the library. Lady Denham, like a true great lady, talked, and talked only of her own concerns, and Charlotte listened. Taking hold of Charlotte's arm with the ease of one who felt that any notice from her was a favour, and communica-

tive from the same sense of importance, or from a
natural love of talking, she immediately said in
a tone of great satisfaction, and with a look of arch
sagacity :—

'Miss Esther wants me to invite her and her
brother to spend a week with me at Sanditon House,
as I did last summer, but I shan't. She has been
trying to get round me every way with her praise
of this and her praise of that ; but I saw what she
was about. I saw through it all. I am not very
easily taken in, my dear.'

Charlotte could think of nothing more harmless to
be said than the simple enquiry of, ' Sir Edward and
Miss Denham ? '

' Yes, my dear ; *my young folks*, as I call them,
sometimes : for I take them very much by the
hand, and had them with me last summer, about
this time, for a week—from Monday to Monday—
and very delighted and thankful they were. For
they are very good young people, my dear. I
would not have you think that I only notice them
for poor dear Sir Harry's sake. No, no ; they are
very deserving themselves, or, trust me, they would
not be so much in my company. I am not the
woman to help anybody blindfold. I always take
care to know what I am about, and who I have to
deal with before I stir a finger. I do not think I was
ever overreached in my life ; and that is a good deal
for a woman to say that has been twice married.
Poor dear Sir Harry (between ourselves) thought

at first to have got more, but (with a bit of a sigh) he is gone, and we must not find fault with the dead. Nobody could live happier together than us : and he was a very honourable man, quite the gentleman, of ancient family ; and when he died I gave Sir Edward his gold watch.'

This was said with a look at her companion which implied its right to produce a great impression ; and seeing no rapturous astonishment in Charlotte's countenance, she added quickly,

' He did not bequeath it to his nephew, my dear ; it was no bequest ; it was not in the will. He only told me, and *that* but *once*, that he should wish his nephew to have his watch ; but it need not have been binding, if I had not chose it.'

' Very kind indeed, very handsome ! ' said Charlotte, absolutely forced to affect admiration.

' Yes, my dear ; and it is not the only kind thing I have done by him. I have been a very liberal friend to Sir Edward ; and, poor young man, he needs it bad enough. For, though I am only the dowager, my dear, and he is the heir, things do not stand between us in the way they usually do between those two parties. Not a shilling do I receive from the Denham estate. Sir Edward has no payments to make *me*. *He* don't stand uppermost, believe me ; it is *I* that help *him*.'

' Indeed ! he is a very fine young man, and particularly elegant in his address.'

This was said chiefly for the sake of saying something ; but Charlotte directly saw that it was laying her open to suspicion, by Lady Denham's giving a shrewd glance at her, and replying,

' Yes, yes ; he's very well to look at ; and it is to be hoped that somebody of large fortune will think so ; for Sir Edward *must* marry for money. He and I often talk that matter over. A handsome young man like him will go smirking and smiling about, and paying girls compliments, but he knows he *must* marry for money. And Sir Edward is a very steady young man, in the main, and has got very good notions.'

' Sir Edward Denham,' said Charlotte, ' with such personal advantages, may be almost sure of getting a woman of fortune, if he chooses it.'

This glorious sentiment seemed quite to remove suspicion.

' Aye, my dear, that is very sensibly said ; and if we could but get a young heiress to Sanditon ! But heiresses are monstrous scarce ! I do not think we have had an heiress here, nor even a *Co.*, since Sanditon has been a public place. Families come after families, but, as far as I can learn, it is not one in a hundred of them that have any real property, landed or funded. An income, perhaps, but no property. Clergymen, may be, or lawyers from town, or half-pay officers, or widows with only a jointure ; and what good can such people do to anybody ? Except just as they take our empty houses, and (between ourselves) I think they are great fools for not staying at home. Now, if we could get a young heiress to be sent here for her health, and, as soon as she got well, have her fall in love with Sir Edward ! And Miss Esther must marry some-body of fortune, too. She must get a rich husband. Ah ! young ladies that have no money are very much to be pitied.' After a short pause : ' If Miss Esther thinks to talk me into inviting them to come and stay at Sanditon House, she will find herself mistaken. Matters are altered with me since last summer, you know : I have Miss Clara with me now, which makes a great difference. I should not choose to have my two housemaid's time taken up all the morning in dusting out bedrooms. They have Miss Clara's room to put to rights, as well as mine, every day. If they had hard work, they would want higher wages.'

Charlotte's feelings were divided between amuse-ment and indignation. She kept her countenance, and kept a civil silence ; but without attempting to listen any longer, and only conscious that Lady Denham was still talking in the same way, allowed her own thoughts to form themselves into such meditation as this :—' She is thoroughly mean ; I had no expectation of anything so bad. Mr. Parker spoke too mildly of her. He is too kind-hearted to see clearly, and their very connection misleads him. He has persuaded her to engage in the same speculation, and because they have so far the same object in view, he fancies that she feels like him in

other things ; but she is very, very mean. I can see
no good in her. Poor Miss Brereton ! And it makes
everybody mean about her. This poor Sir Edward
and his sister ! how far nature meant them to be
respectable I cannot tell ; but they are obliged to be
mean in their servility to her ; and I am mean, too,
in giving her my attention with the appearance of
coinciding with her. Thus it is when rich people are
sordid.'

Mr. Parker has two unmarried sisters of singu-
lar character. They live together ; Diana, the
younger, always takes the lead, and the elder follows
in the same track. It is their pleasure to fancy
themselves invalids to a degree and in a manner
never experienced by others ; but, from a state of
exquisite pain and utter prostration, Diana Parker
can always rise to be officious in the concerns of all
her acquaintance, and to make incredible exertions
where they are not wanted.

It would seem that they must be always either
very busy for the good of others, or else extremely
ill themselves. Some natural delicacy of constitution, in fact, with an unfortunate turn for medicine,
especially quack medicine, had given them an early
tendency at various times to various disorders. The
rest of their suffering was from their own fancy, the
love of distinction, and the love of the wonderful.
They had charitable hearts and many amiable feelings ; but a spirit of restless activity, and the glory
of doing more than anybody else, had a share in

every exertion of benevolence, and there was vanity in all they did, as well as in all they endured.

These peculiarities come out in the following letter of Diana Parker to her brother :—

' MY DEAR TOM,—We were much grieved at your accident, and if you had not described yourself as having fallen into such very good hands, I should have been with you at all hazards the day after receipt of your letter, though it found me suffering under a more severe attack than usual of my old grievance, spasmodic bile, and hardly able to crawl from my bed to the sofa. But how were you treated ? Send me more particulars in your next. If indeed a simple sprain, as you denominate it, nothing would have been so judicious as friction— friction by the hand alone, supposing it could be applied *immediately*. Two years ago I happened to be calling on Mrs. Sheldon, when her coachman sprained his foot, as he was cleaning the carriage, and could hardly limp into the house ; but by the immediate use of friction alone, steadily persevered in (I rubbed his ancle with my own hands for four hours without intermission), he was well in three days. . . . Pray never run into peril again in looking for an apothecary on our account ; for had you the most experienced man in his line settled at Sanditon, it would be no recommendation to us. We have entirely done with the whole medical tribe. We have consulted physician after physician in vain, till we are quite convinced that they can do nothing for us, and that we must trust to our knowledge of our own wretched constitutions for any relief ; but if you think it advisable for the interests of the *place* to get a medical man there, I will undertake the commission with pleasure, and have no doubt of succeeding. I could soon put the necessary irons in the fire. As for getting to Sanditon myself, it is an impossibility. I grieve to say that I cannot attempt it, but my feelings tell me too plainly that in my present state the sea-air would probably be the death of me ; and in truth I doubt whether Susan's nerves would be equal to the effort. She has been suffering much from headache, and six leeches a day, for ten days together, relieved her so little that we thought it right to change our measures ; and being convinced on examination that much of the evil lay in her gums, I persuaded her to attack the disorder there. She has accordingly had three teeth drawn, and is decidedly better ; but her nerves are a good deal deranged, she can only speak in a whisper, and fainted away this morning on poor Arthur's trying to suppress a cough.'

Within a week of the date of this letter, in spite of the impossibility of moving, and of the fatal effects to be apprehended from the sea-air, Diana Parker was at Sanditon with her sister. She had flattered herself that by her own indefatigable exertions, and by setting at work the agency of many friends, she had induced two large families to take houses at Sanditon. It was to expedite these politic views that she came ; and though she met with some disappointment of her expectation, yet she did not suffer in health.

Such were some of the *dramatis personæ*, ready dressed and prepared for their parts. They are at least original and unlike any that the author had produced before. The success of the piece must have depended on the skill with which these parts might be played ; but few will be inclined to distrust the skill of one who had so often succeeded. If the author had lived to complete her work, it is probable that these personages might have grown into as mature an individuality of character, and have taken as permanent a place amongst our familiar acquaintance, as Mr. Bennet, or John Thorp, Mary Musgrove, or Aunt Norris herself.

CHAPTER XIV.

Postscript.

WHEN first I was asked to put together a memoir of my aunt, I saw reasons for declining the attempt. It was not only that, having passed the three score years and ten usually allotted to man's strength, and being unaccustomed to write for publication, I might well distrust my ability to complete the work, but that I also knew the extreme scantiness of the materials out of which it must be constructed. The grave closed over my aunt fifty-two years ago ; and during that long period no idea of writing her life had been entertained by any of her family. Her nearest relatives, far from making provision for such a purpose, had actually destroyed many of the letters and papers by which it might have been facilitated. They were influenced, I believe, partly by an extreme dislike to publishing private details, and partly by never having assumed that the world would take so strong and abiding an interest in her works as to claim her name as public property. It was therefore necessary for me to draw upon recollections rather than on written documents for my materials ; while the subject itself supplied me with nothing striking or prominent with which to arrest the attention of the reader. It has been said that the happiest individuals, like nations during their happiest periods, have no history. In the case of my aunt, it was not only that her course of life was unvaried, but that her own disposition was remarkably calm and even. There was in her nothing eccentric or angular; no ruggedness of temper; no singularity of manner; none of the morbid sensibility or exaggeration of feeling, which not unfrequently accompanies great talents, to be worked up into a picture. Hers was a mind well balanced on a basis of good sense, sweetened by an affectionate heart, and regulated by fixed principles; so that she was to be distinguished from many other amiable and sensible women only by that peculiar genius which shines out clearly enough in her works, but of which a biographer can make little use. The motive which at last induced me to make the attempt is exactly expressed in the passage prefixed to these pages. I thought that I saw something to be done: knew of no one who could do it but myself, and so was driven to the enterprise. I am glad that I have been able to finish my work. As a family record it can scarcely fail to be interesting to those relatives who must ever set a high value on their connection with Jane Austen, and to them I especially dedicate it; but as I have been asked to do so, I also submit it to the censure of the public, with all its faults both of deficiency and redundancy. I know that its value in their eyes must depend, not on any merits of its own, but on the degree of estimation in which my aunt's works may still be held ; and indeed I shall esteem it one of the strongest testimonies ever borne to her talents, if for her sake an interest can be taken in so poor a sketch as I have been able to draw.

Bray Vicarage:
Sept. 7, 1869.

Postscript printed at the end of the first edition ; omitted from the second.

Since these pages were in type, I have read with astonishment the strange misrepresentation of my aunt's manners given by Miss Mitford in a letter which appears in her lately-published Life, vol. i. p. 305. Miss Mitford does not profess to have known Jane Austen herself, but to report what had been told her by her mother. Having stated that her mother ' *before her marriage* ' was well acquainted with Jane Austen and her family, she writes thus :—' Mamma says that she was *then* the prettiest, silliest, most affected, husband-hunting butterfly she ever remembers.' The editor of Miss Mitford's Life very properly observes in a note how different this description is from

'every other account of Jane Austen from whatever quarter.' Certainly it is so totally at variance
with the modest simplicity of character which I
have attributed to my aunt, that if it could be
supposed to have a semblance of truth, it must be
equally injurious to her memory and to my
trustworthiness as her biographer. Fortunately I
am not driven to put my authority in competition
with that of Miss Mitford, nor to ask which ought
to be considered the better witness in this case ;
because I am able to prove by a reference to dates
that Miss Mitford must have been under a mistake,
and that her mother could not possibly have known
what she was supposed to have reported ; inasmuch as Jane Austen, at the time referred to, was
a little girl.

Mrs. Mitford was the daughter of Dr. Russell,
Rector of Ashe, a parish adjoining Steventon, so
that the families of Austen and Russell must at
that time have been known to each other. But
the date assigned by Miss Mitford for the termina-
tion of the acquaintance is the time of her mother's
marriage. This took place in October 1785, when
Jane, who had been born in December 1775, was
not quite ten years old. In point of fact, however,
Miss Russell's opportunities of observing Jane
Austen must have come to an end still earlier : for
upon Dr. Russell's death, in January 1783, his
widow and daughter removed from the neighbourhood, so that all intercourse between the families

ceased when Jane was little more than seven years old.

All persons who undertake to narrate from hearsay things which are supposed to have taken place before they were born are liable to error, and are apt to call in imagination to the aid of memory : and hence it arises that many a fancy piece has been substituted for genuine history.

I do not care to correct the inaccurate account of Jane Austen's manners in after life : because Miss Mitford candidly expresses a doubt whether she had not been misinformed on that point.

Nov. 17, 1869.

NOTES

NOTES

CHAPTER I

Page 4 l. 8 from foot. *Deane and Steventon.* Mr. Austen became Rector of Steventon 1761, of Deane not until 1773. *Life* p. 17.

Page 6 l. 5. *Letters to and from Samuel Johnson* (1788) ii. 245. Mrs. Piozzi prints ' eighty-six years old ' and ' replied the Master dryly '.

Page 7 l. 10 from foot. *Deane.* See the note to page 4.
    l. 7 from foot. *son of . . . Warren Hastings.* This is very doubtful ; see *Life* p. 10. Mr. Austen-Leigh suspects a confusion with Hastings de Feuillide, who undoubtedly did stay at Steventon and did die young.

Page 8 l. 10. *Mary Russell Mitford.* See p. 209 for the strictures on Miss Mitford, which were suppressed in the second edition.

Page 9 l. 5. *1771.* See the note to p. 4.

Page 11 l. 1. *a century ago.* Percy told Johnson ' that it might be discerned whether or no there was a clergyman resident in a parish by the civil or savage manner of the people ' (Hill's Boswell, iii. 437). Sir Thomas Bertram's opinion on the duty of residence will be remembered.

Page 16 l. 17. *Mrs. Latournelle.* Her real name was Sarah Hackett. *Gentleman's Magazine* 1797 p. 983.

CHAPTER II

Page 20 l. 2. *One who knew and loved it well.* There is reason to suspect that the lines here quoted are by the writer's father, Jane Austen's brother James. A manuscript collection of verses by him, now in the possession of Captain Ernest Austen, R.N., contains a poem in blank verse, signed J. A. and dated July 1814, which describes, among other matters, the beauties of the Steventon country.

These are thy charms, my native valley ; these
Thy beauties ;　artless, but possessing much
The power of sweet attraction to my heart.

Another part of England is condemned, on the ground that

to the eye of cultured taste, that dwells
On Nature's sketches picturesque and wild,
'Tis unproductive, waste, and barren all.

The manuscript does not contain the lines beginning

True taste is not fastidious.

But the poem may have contained them.　For the manuscript is defective, probably by a pair of leaves (for the hiatus is in the middle of a quire).　The result is that a poem in octosyllabics called Morning, and addressed to Edward (i. e. J. E. A.-L.), ends in the middle of a sentence ;　and the following poem, described above, is defective at the beginning.　It is tempting to guess that the missing leaves contained our five lines.　They may have been detached for copying, and so mislaid.

I owe this brilliant conjecture to Miss Jean Smith.

Page 25 l. 2.　*I believe.*　See p. 75 for positive evidence of a visit to Bath about Jan. 1798.

l. 2 from foot.　*Feuillade* should be *Feuillide*.　The first edition has Fieuillade, which might arise from misunderstanding of a proof-correction.

Page 26.　For a more accurate account see *Life* p. 44.

Page 27 l. 16.　*engaged.*　To the Rev. Thomas Fowle, who died 1797.　His noble relative was Lord Craven.

Page 29 l. 20.　*could* is accidentally omitted in the second edition.

Page 34 l. 7.　The quotation appears, in a slightly different form, in *The Antiquary*, ch. xi.　I have not been able to trace it.

Page 40 l. 14.　*Trivia.*　See the end of Book I.

CHAPTER III

Page 61 l. 5 from foot. I have restored *which* from the original.

Page 62 l. 4. *Marcau.* J. A. wrote *Marcou.* St. Marcouf is the name of two small islands off Normandy, then occupied by the British.

Page 64 l. 1. *maple.* J. A. wrote ' maypole '.
l. 12. This is the letter which was sent by Francis Austen (Martha Lloyd became his second wife in 1828) to the Boston admirer of the novels. See p. 152.
l. 6 of the letter. J. A. always wrote *Ibthrop.* The pronunciation is *Ibtrop*, like *Altrop* for *Althorp.*

Page 66 l. 14. J. A. wrote *disultary.*

Page 69 l. 1. *gold chains and topaze crosses.* The crosses, and this letter, were until recently preserved in the donor's family. They lately changed hands, but are still together, and as the authenticity of the crosses depends upon their pedigree, it is to be hoped that the letter will always be kept with them.
Readers of *Mansfield Park* will not need to be reminded of the amber cross which William Price sent to Fanny.

CHAPTER IV

Page 70 l. 2. *Sydney Terrace* should be Sydney Place.

Page 72 l. 8. *for a few months.* Actually from March 1805 to July 1806.
l. 2 of the letter. J. A. wrote ' this fine striped paper '.

Page 79 l. 5. *L. L.* J. A. wrote ' Lucy Lefroy '.
l. 4 from foot. *Blashford.* J. A. wrote *Blachford.*

Page 80 l. 12. J. A. wrote ' tell a lie himself '.

Page 82 l. 1. *end of 1805.* See note to p. 72.
l. 2. *Southampton.* From autumn of 1806 to March 1809.
l. 6. *four years.* Actually two and a half.

Page 83 foot-note. The note by Thomas Warton (not Wharton) first appears in the 1778 edition of Johnson-Steevens. It justifies the correction ' Hampton pier ' for the ' Dover pier ' of the folios (*Henry V* iii. 1).

CHAPTER V

Page 89 last line. *Mrs. Crabbe.* In a letter of 1813 J. A. had ' only just been making out from one of his prefaces that he probably was married '.

Page 90 l. 5. *Only three.* Actually four—*Waverley, Guy Mannering, The Antiquary,* and the First Series (1816) of *Tales of my Landlord.*

l. 12. From a letter to Anna Austen (see below) of 28 Sept. 1814 (*Brabourne* ii. 315, *Life* 359). ' Mrs. ——'s ' is ' Mrs. West's Alicia de Lacy ' (of which, since my edition of the novels, I have found a record ; it was published in 1814). ' E.' should naturally refer to Edward (i. e. J. E. A.-L., the author of the *Memoir*) ; but J. A. wrote ' yours ', in reference to Anna's performance.

l. 5 from foot. *two of her nieces.* These were Jane Anna Elizabeth (Lefroy), always known as Anna, and her half-sister Caroline, daughters of James Austen. The two extracts on pp. 90–91 are Caroline's, that on pp. 91–92 is Anna's.

Page 92 l. 5. *seventeen years.* Anna was born in April 1793, her aunt in December 1775.

Page 94. Both extracts are from letters to Anna. The first is from a letter of 29 Nov. 1814 (*Brabourne* ii. 321, *Life* 361, misdated 28 Nov.—the performance of *Isabella* at Covent Garden was on Monday 28 Nov.). The second is from an undated scrap (*Brabourne* ii. 323, *Life* 362 ; Lord B. attached it to a letter to which it does not belong). Miss B. is Miss Blachford, mentioned p. 79 above.

l. 2. *Isabella, or the Fatal Marriage,* a tragedy adapted by Garrick from Southerne.

Page 96. For a fuller text of these letters to Anna, see Lord Brabourne's second volume, or *Life* pp. 354–362. ' Your aunt C.' is of course Cassandra.

Page 97 l. 2. J. A. wrote ' Forrester's '.
l. 23. *your husband.* J. A. wrote ' Ben '.

Page 98 l. 7. *A specimen.* I have not included this facsimile, which is not very well executed.

CHAPTER VI

Page 103 l. 15. *till* ed. 1 : *till*, ed. 2.
l. 19. *Egerton.* T. Egerton, of the Military Library, Whitehall.

Page 104 l. 12 of the letter. *Miss B.* is Miss Benn.
l. 3 from foot. *typical* is not a mistake, as might be supposed, for *typographical* ; see quotations in the Oxford Dictionary.

Page 105 l. 1. *Marmion* vi. 38 :

> ' I do not rhyme to that dull elf
> Who cannot image to himself.'

l. 3 from foot. J. A. wrote *anything*, not *something*.

Page 106 l. 2. This misprint is on p. 220 of the third volume, l. 5 from the foot, at the end of chapter 12 (54 in most editions). The two speeches are : (Jane) ' How hard it is in some cases to be believed ! ' (Elizabeth) ' And how impossible in others ! '
l. 7. *The following letter.* The author must have mixed his extracts ; for what follows is made up of parts of two letters, of 24 Jan. and 9 Feb. See *Life* 258. The passage beginning ' Our party on Wednesday ' and ending ' another fortnight if necessary ', and the last two sentences, ' I have learned . . . Commissioner's ', belong to the letter of 24 Jan. ; the remainder to that of 9 Feb.
l. 4 from foot. *Mrs.* —— is Mrs. Digweed.
l. 3 from foot. *Rejected Addresses* was published in 1812.

Page 107 l. 13. *a Society octavo.* The *Society* was the Reading Club at Chawton.
Military Police. J. A. no doubt wrote *Policy* ; the book is not about policemen.
l. 19. *Clarkson or Buchanan.* For these obscure authors the curious may consult the index of literary allusions in my edition of the novels.

l. 8 from foot. Mrs. Anne Grant, *Letters from the Mountains* (1807).

Page 108 l. 2. J. A. wrote ' lay in her house '.
l. 11. *their society* might be read as meaning ' the society of quartos ', though that makes nonsense of the following *They*. J. A. wrote ' their Society ' meaning the Reading Club at Manydown, where Cassandra was staying.
l. 15. *the Commissioner's.* William Price speaks of the *coiffure* of ' Mrs. Brown, and the other women, at the Commissioner's, at Gibraltar '. *Mansfield Park* Vol. II ch. 6 (ch. 24 in most editions).

Page 110 l. 20. J. A. wrote ' with the front drawing-room all to myself '.

Page 112 l. 3. J. A. wrote ' very different '.
l. 10. *the " Heroine ".* The Heroine, or the Adventures of Cherubina (1813) by Eaton Stannard Barrett. The late Sir Walter Raleigh (agreeing with J. A. against her brother James) persuaded the Oxford Press to reprint this book, and it may be read in the *Oxford Miscellany.*
l. 23. *M^{d.} B.* Madame Bigeon, Henry Austen's servant, to whom J. A. left a legacy of £50.

Page 114 l. 1. *little Cass.* Doubtless one of the nieces of that name, then staying at the Great House.
l. 5. J. A. wrote *Gogmagoglicus.*

CHAPTER VII

Page 117 l. 7. *worthy* ed. 1 : *worth* ed. 2.

Page 120 l. 7 from foot. *Beattie's Minstrel* I 16. The misquotation, *in his looks* for *now his look*, is not Mr. Clarke's.
l. 2 from foot. *La Fontaine.* The reference is to the French translation, *Nouveaux Tableaux de Famille* (reprinted in London 1803), of August Lafontaine's *Leben eines armes Landpredigers,* 1801.

Page 122 l. 2. *inferior in good sense.* J. A. wrote ' very inferior in good sense '.

Page 125 l. 3. *Two Gentlemen of Verona* II. vii. ' free course ' should be ' fair course '.

l. 8 from foot. The quotation from Mrs. Gaskell is substantially accurate, except that ' Whenever I *do* ' should be ' If I ever *do* ' and that ' its way ' should be ' its own way '.

Page 126. For a full text and facsimile of the *Plan* see *Plan of a Novel* &c. (Oxford 1926). The *Plan* should be read with the full text of the correspondence with Mr. Clarke which suggested it. James Stanier Clarke (who was probably some ten years Miss Austen's senior) was at one time a naval chaplain. He became in 1799 domestic chaplain to the Prince of Wales. He published lives of James II and of Nelson, and an edition of Falconer's *Shipwreck.*

The author of the Memoir has obscured the connexion of the *Plan* with Mr. Clarke's letters, by omitting from the correspondence most of the points which appear in the *Plan*, and from the *Plan* most of the points which come from the letters. He retains the ' invectives against the holders of tithes ' (p. 128 *sub fin.*) but without explanation. I conjecture that he had not seen Mr. Clarke's letter of December 1815 (p. 29 of the Oxford edition of the *Plan*) and left out certain sentences of the *Plan* because he did not understand the allusion.

Page 132 l. 10 from foot. *the late event* was Henry Austen's bankruptcy in March 1816.

CHAPTER VIII

Page 137 last line. *The fate of ' Northanger Abbey'.* For the whole story see *Life* 230–234. *Susan* was sold, not to a publisher in Bath, but to Messrs. Crosbie & Co. of London, from whom it was recovered in 1809. The copy of J. A.'s letter to Crosbie, and the reply, are now in the British Museum. In its original form the book was written in 1797–8 ; the *Advertisement by the Authoress* prefixed to it in 1818 describes it as ' finished in the year 1803 ' and as ' made comparatively obsolete ' by the lapse of thirteen years. Publication was intended, therefore, in 1816. But on 13 March 1817 J. A. wrote that ' *Miss Catherine* is put upon the shelf for the present '.

Page 138 l. 13. *One of her brothers.* The first edition names him as ' Mr. Henry Austen '.

Page 139 l. 8. A fragment of a letter, Dec. 1814, to Anna Lefroy. ' Mr. C.' should be ' Mrs. Creed '. The list is preserved (see below, note on p. 150). Mrs. Creed's opinion as recorded is simply that she preferred *Sense and Sensibility* and *Pride and Prejudice*. The original of this letter is mutilated, so that we do not know who ' Mr. D.' was.

l. 12. *Self-Control.* A novel by Mrs. Brunton (1810). In a letter of 11 Oct. 1813 J. A. describes it as ' an excellently-meant, elegantly-written work, without anything of nature or probability in it '.

l. 17. Another fragment of a letter to Anna Lefroy. *Rosanne ; or a Father's Labour Lost* is a novel (1814) by Laetitia Matilda Hawkins, daughter of the notorious Sir John Hawkins, the official biographer of Johnson.

Page 140 note. J. E. A.-L. was unaware that the *earlier* of the two *Quarterly* reviews *was* by Scott. See *Life* 326, where the attribution is given on the authority of the present Mr. John Murray. The review was of *Emma,* which was published early in 1816. (The *Quarterly* for October 1815 did not appear until March 1816.)

CHAPTER IX

Page 146 l. 14. *the ' Keepsake ' of 1825.* The date is 1835.

Page 147 l. 3. *clear style.* Misprinted ' dear style ' in all editions.

Page 149 l. 8. *finely written.* Scott wrote ' very finely written '.

Page 150. For the *Opinions* on *Mansfield Park* and *Emma* see the *Life* 328–332. The full text, with facsimiles of the originals, is in *Plan of a Novel* &c. (Oxford 1926).

Page 152 l. 16. *a long letter of his sister's.* This was the letter to Martha Lloyd, Sir Francis's second wife, which is printed on p. 64. It is in the possession of Mrs. M. A. De Wolfe Howe of Boston, a member of the Quincey family.

CHAPTER X

Page 157 l. 7 from foot. *Jemima.* Anna Jemima, eldest daughter of Ben and Anna Lefroy, was born 20 Oct. 1815.

Page 158 l. 8. *one pound* should no doubt be 'one guinea' (worth at that date 21*s*.). Until the abolition of the guinea in 1816, though money was reckoned in 'pounds', payment could only be made in 'guineas'.

CHAPTER XI

Page 159 l. 5. *distant friends.* The distance between Chawton and Kintbury is not very great. Mr. Onions of the Oxford Dictionary confirms my conjecture that 'distant friends' means 'distant relatives'. Eliza Lloyd, elder sister of Martha and Mary, married a Mr. Fowle.

l. 15. The letter to Charles is now in the British Museum (*Life* 385). J. A. actually wrote 'I am the only one of the Legatees who has been so silly'. The disappointment consisted partly in postponement, the legacies being subject to a life interest.

l. 20. *another correspondent.* This is from the letter printed by Henry Austen in his *Biographical Notice of the Author* prefixed in 1818 to *Northanger Abbey and Persuasion.* The reference is to the disappointment mentioned above. The letter is quoted again on p. 174.

Page 160 l. 6. *a nephew.* James Edward Austen-Leigh, the author of the *Memoir*, who was known as Edward Austen when his uncle and cousin had both become Edward Knight.

Page 161 l. 2. *Mary Jane.* Francis Austen's eldest daughter, then nine years old.

Page 162 l. 3. J. A. wrote 'improvements', which is a technical term of landscape gardening. In *She Stoops to Conquer* (i. 1) 'My aunt's bell rings for our afternoon's walk round the improvements'.

Page 164 l. 10. *vigorous.* J. A. wrote 'spirited'.
l. 13. *as produces.* J. A. wrote 'as to produce'.

Page 165 l. 9. *Amiable.* J. A. wrote Aimable'.

Page 166 l. 10. *Persuasion.* See the text of the cancelled chapter (p. 177) and the note.

Page 170 l. 14. *her niece.* Caroline. For this letter see *Life* 170.

Page 171 l. 6. *my father.* James Austen inherited a large sum from Mr. Leigh Perrot, subject to the widow's life-interest.

Page 174 l. 4. *a confirmation.* J. A. wrote ' which is confirmation '.

l. 19. *before printed.* See note to p. 159 l. 20.

Page 175 l. 2. *clergymen.* James and Henry.

CHAPTER XII

Page 177. See the Oxford edition (1926) of *Two Chapters of Persuasion* (from the MS. now in the British Museum). They were the tenth and eleventh of the second volume as originally planned. The tenth was replaced by two chapters, 10 and 11, and the concluding chapter became 12. The original 10 was not, as is stated on p. 166, entirely cancelled ; a considerable part of it was retained almost verbatim. The author of the *Memoir*, by an odd confusion of thought, sometimes accommodated the text of this part to the revised version printed in 1818. But the variations are unimportant, so that this does not much matter ; and they are here ignored. I call attention however to a few misprints or errors of transcription in the text of 1871.

Page 178, last lines. J. A. wrote ' Aye, aye, that will do. Now, it is right. I *thought*, we were not mistaken.' The punctuation of 1871 perverts the sense ; the Admiral is not comforting Anne, but triumphing in his own penetration.

Page 180 l. 9. *arose, again to entreat.* J. A. wrote ' arose again—to entreat '.

Page 181 l. 8. *disturbed.* J. A. wrote ' distressed '.

Page 184 l. 4. After *your message* the MS. has ' This was spoken, as with a fortitude which seemed to meet the message '. This was omitted in 1871 by an accident of a very common kind ; the eye of the copyist or the printer jumped from the first *message* to the second.

l. 8 from foot. *on his supplication.* J. A. wrote ' on his side, Supplication '.

l. 5 from foot. *in all the fulness.* J. A. wrote ' in the fullness '.

Page 187 l. 6 from foot. *concerning them.* J. A. wrote ' concerning him '.

Page 188 l. 4. *Bath—Bath had instantly followed.* The punctuation obscures the sense. J. A. wrote ' Bath, Bath—had instantly followed ', quoting F. W.'s *thought.* (Originally she wrote ' To Bath, To Bath '.)

l. 8. *the morning's.* J. A. wrote ' this morning's '.

l. 3 from foot. *support.* J. A. wrote ' supports '.

Page 190 l. 7. *divided.* J. A. wrote ' decided '.

CHAPTER XIII

Page 192. *The Last Work.* This fragment, traditionally known as *Sanditon,* was first completely published by the present editor (Oxford 1925). The extracts in the *Memoir* are not given *verbatim.*

l. 16. *first traced in pencil.* The inference here drawn is not borne out by inspection of the MS. The pencil passage is not in fact much later than the middle ; and what is written later, in ink, is no less well written than the early pages.

Page 198 l. 9. *chamber horse.* A mechanical contrivance for taking exercise indoors. The MS. seems to have *house* (and it is so printed in the Oxford edition of 1925) ; but there can hardly be a doubt that J. A. intended *horse.*

CHAPTER XIV

Page 207 l. 7. *scantiness of the materials.* The author was unaware of the existence of the letters afterwards (1884) published by Lord Brabourne ; see Lord B.'s preface.

INDEX

HER CHARACTER AND OPINIONS :

Her person, 87 ; Cassandra's drawing, the frontispiece to the *Memoir*, 88 ; accomplishments, 88 ; skill with her fingers, 97 ; love of dancing, 33 ; of the Navy, 15 ; opinions on history and literature, 89 ; on acting, 94 ; on novel-writing, 96 ; on Johnson, Crabbe, Cowper, Scott, Miss Edgeworth, 89–90 ; happy temper, 2, 17 ; to know her was to love her, 82 ; the delight of her nephews and nieces, 2, 90–92 ; rectitude and delicacy, 99 ; freedom from eccentricity, 208 ; religion, 100, 175 ; humility, 174 ; love of the ridiculous, 92.

AS AUTHOR :

Habits of composition, 97, 102 ; ' three or four families in a country village is the very thing to work on ', 96 ; ' the little bit (two inches wide) of ivory ', 164 ; an ' unlearned and uninformed female ', 122 ; fear of overwriting herself, 134 ; avoidance of matters she did not understand, 15, 122, 124 ; thought by Whately to be ' a female writing from recollection ', 28 ; her characters not drawn from individuals, 156 ; ' the brilliant girl and the mature woman ' (the early and the later novels), 155.

HER WORKS :

Sense and Sensibility (published Nov. 1811 ; second edition 1813). ' Something similar ' written earlier and called *Elinor and Marianne*, 49. ' Begun in its present form ' Nov. 1797, 49. Revised at Chawton,